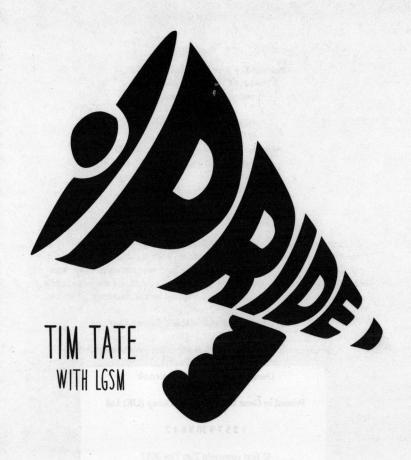

PRIDE

TIM TATE
WITH LGSM

JB
JOHN BLAKE

Published by John Blake Publishing Ltd,
3 Bramber Court, 2 Bramber Road,
London W14 9PB, England

www.johnblakebooks.com

www.facebook.com/johnblakebooks [f]
twitter.com/jblakebooks [t]

This edition published in 2017

ISBN: 978 1 78 606 291 8

British Library Cataloguing-in-Publication Data:

A catalogue record for this book is available from the British Library.

The right of .... asserted by
him .... 988.

Papers use .... ade from
wood gro .... m to the
....

Every attempt has been made to contact the relevant copyright-holders, but some
were unobtainable. We would be grateful if the appropriate people could contact us.

John Blake Publishing is an imprint of Bonnier Publishing
www.bonnierpublishing.com

'Shall the miners be beaten by starvation? Shall the cry of a child for food break the hearts of Britain's strongest men?'

'One of the reasons I support miners is that they dig coal … they go down and do it. I mean, would you go down a mine and work?'

'Dykes + faggots say "Right On, Arthur"'

PREFACE

It was past midnight and they were lost.

The two ancient and battered mini-buses had set out from London many hours before. The twenty-seven gay men and women inside had passed much of the journey singing or leaning out of the windows and blowing flamboyant kisses at other motorists.

Now they were off the motorways and main roads, making a tortuous and erratic journey along dark and deserted lanes. They were searching for Onllwyn, a tiny dot on the map in one of the remotest valleys on the western edge of the South Wales coalfield; a very traditional mining stronghold, in the middle of the most bitterly fought strike for two generations.

They were young, idealistic and metropolitan. They were also openly – and obviously – 'out'. They felt like strangers in an alien landscape. And they were nervous. Very nervous.

On the journey itself there was that sense of adventure but there was also this sinking feeling. We were thinking, 'What the fuck are we doing here?' Because this was unknown territory: the people in the valleys could have been a whole lot of screaming homophobes.

I was super-excited; but also I felt a certain amount of anxiety. We didn't dress like the people in South Wales: we had that 'London look' of the time. Fashion-wise, we certainly didn't look like we came from the valleys.

I thought, 'Jesus, this is going to be interesting.' I was this ingénue; this 'Thoroughly Modern Millie' type of person. I'd only told my parents I was gay less than a year ago – now I was going to a mining village as an open homosexual.

It was past midnight. They were lost. And ahead of them stretched a weekend that would change the life of the beleaguered mining communities of the Dulais Valley – and help end centuries of persecution endured by gay men and lesbian women throughout Britain.

No pressure then.

CONTENTS

INTRODUCTION

This book tells the story of one of the most unlikely alliances in living memory.

In 1984 and 1985 a small group of metropolitan homosexual men and lesbian women stepped away from the vibrant hedonism of London's gay scene to befriend and support the beleaguered villages of a very traditional mining community in the remote valleys of South Wales.

They did so in the midst of the most divisive strike in two generations and in one of the most turbulent times in modern British history. Five years earlier, Margaret Thatcher's Conservative government had begun a radical programme to change the way the country had lived since the end of World War Two. That cosy, consensual 'One Nation' approach to politics was to be replaced with an unforgivingly right-wing approach: there was, in Mrs Thatcher's own words, 'no such thing as society.' Henceforth, greed was not just good but God: making money was more important than making things, private profit was put before public need and, above all, the costs of change were to be borne by those least able to afford them.

Traditional manufacturing industries were sacrificed on the altar of the free market; unemployment rose inexorably and, across the north of England, Scotland and Wales, community after community became – as a 1981 No.1 pop song bleakly observed – a 'Ghost Town'. Simultaneously, the previously lukewarm Cold War re-froze as American nuclear missiles arrived on air bases across the country.

The Thatcher revolution was profoundly unpopular. Opposition and anger mounted; riots erupted in cities across Britain. The governmental response was to increase state surveillance and police harassment. For those who lived through the early years of the 1980s, fear – of poverty, of unemployment, of the authorities and of nuclear war – was a very real and constant presence.

Conflict was, perhaps, inevitable: certainly, the government had planned for it. In 1984 it erupted: twenty-two months after defeating an external enemy – Argentina – in the Falklands, Mrs Thatcher and her allies declared war on what the Prime Minister described as 'the enemy within' – the men whose labour powered Britain's homes and industry. The year-long miners' strike was the longest and most bitterly fought industrial dispute since the 1926 General Strike. It divided the country, was marred by violence and devastated previously thriving mining communities.

That the government was – in its mind – engaged in an existential fight against a powerful foe was confirmed by one of the ministers most closely involved: the Energy Secretary described preparations for the battles to come as 'just like re-arming to face the threat of Hitler in the 1930s.' And, just as in 1939, all the powers of the State were to be focused on ensuring victory.

But the early 1980s was also a period in which another oppressed group came under renewed and sustained attack. After hundreds of years of persecution, homosexuality had been decriminalised in England and Wales in 1967 – though, as we shall see, in reality gay men and lesbian women still faced discrimination and were frequently harassed.

The 1967 Sexual Offences Act removed the threat of imprisonment for gay men (lesbians were, as they had been throughout history, largely ignored) – at least in limited circumstances. It became safer – if not always safe – to 'come out': as a result, gay communities emerged from their previous shadowy existence. Openly gay pubs and clubs did good business and, in London and the bigger cities at least, a sometimes ecstatically sybaritic nightlife flourished. In 1978 the Tom Robinson Band's unequivocally defiant anthem, 'Glad to Be Gay', spent weeks in the Top 20.

But if homosexuality was now the love which dared to broadcast its name, the endemic prejudice against it had not gone away. The BBC refused to broadcast Robinson's song in its Top 40 chart show. More seriously, many gay men still found themselves in court after being arrested by undercover police, while others received a criminal record for having the temerity to kiss their partners in public. 'Queer-bashing' remained a very real threat and high-profile prosecutions targeted some of the nascent community's most important supporting organisations.

And then AIDS arrived in Britain.

In 1981 a forty-nine-year-old man was admitted to London's Brompton Hospital suffering from pneumocystis carinii pneumonia (PCP). He died ten days later, becoming the country's first known death from HIV/AIDS. By 1983 there were seventeen reported cases and the long-simmering prejudice against homosexuality re-surfaced. National newspapers ran endless stories about 'the gay plague', and public and religious leaders pronounced the disease to be 'God's punishment' on gay men for their 'sinful' lifestyle. Homophobia was re-legitimised.

At the very height of this perfect storm, as the government and police battled 'the enemy within' in communities across the land, and as newspapers whipped up fear of the 'perverts' who had (supposedly) inflicted this lethal new pestilence upon the entire population, two groups who ostensibly had nothing in common – miners and homosexuals – unexpectedly made both common cause and lasting friendship.

It was an alliance that helped keep an entire valley clothed and fed during the darkest months of the strike, and it led directly to a long-overdue acceptance by trades unions and the Labour Party that homosexual equality was a cause to be championed.

The story of that seemingly unlikely alliance between the

stylish young metropolitans of Lesbians and Gays Support the Miners (LGSM) and the very traditional Welsh mining communities of the Neath, Dulais and Upper Swansea Valleys was told in the 2014 feature film *Pride*.

The movie – a relatively low-budget British production – was screened at the Cannes Film Festival and was nominated for both the Golden Globes and BAFTA Awards. Part *Billy Elliot*, part *Brassed Off*, reviews described it as 'a rom-com between two communities' and praised it as 'impassioned and lovable', 'indescribably wonderful' and 'irresistible'. And so it was: *Pride* was all of those things – and much more besides.

This book began life as a companion to the movie. For years the story of LGSM and the South Wales miners had passed beyond memory into folk-myth. Even the creators of *Pride* did not initially believe that the events it depicts could have happened. It is a tribute to them – but more crucially to the men and women of LGSM and the Dulais Valley – that the film stays so close to the historical truth.

But as popular as *Pride* became, and as effectively as it brought the legend to life to a diverse modern audience for whom homophobic discrimination has been vanquished by equal-rights legislation and for whom coal mining is something to be studied in history classes, there was – there is – much more of the story yet to be told. There is much more to discover about how two different communities – each struggling to overcome its own bitter internal arguments and long-established fault lines, as well as facing the power of a hostile government – would find common cause against the odds. And much more to discover about how one simple but unlikely act of friendship would, in time, help change life in Britain forever.

This book aims to tell all of those stories. In it you will meet (almost) all of the real-life characters who made *Pride*, the movie, such a moving and enriching experience. I have been immensely privileged to meet them before you.

Each of the members of LGSM and every one of those from the former mining communities of South Wales who agreed to be interviewed is a remarkable individual: as two separate communities they were extraordinary, and as one passionate unified front in the fight to protect themselves from Margaret Thatcher's war on the miners they were inspiring. Spending the past year in their company has been one of the most rewarding times of my writing life.

I was not, in many ways, the most obvious choice to write this book. As a middle-class, straight Englishman, I cannot claim anything more than an emotional and political kinship with the men and women of this story. Unlike them, I have never been persecuted for my sexuality. I have not had my livelihood torn from me, nor my community destroyed by government diktat. My sole contributions to the struggles recounted in this book were once publicly challenging Margaret Thatcher to endorse gay rights (at a 1978 Conservative Party conference: not a success), and to pitching pound coins into the collection buckets shaken and rattled by striking miners on the streets of London throughout 1984. Neither qualifies me as a genuine foot soldier in what were, unquestionably, vitally important wars.

For that reason, the format of this book is unusual. We

decided collectively that this story is owned by the men and women of LGSM and the Dulais Valley and that, therefore, it should be told by them – directly, in their own words, with as little mediation from me, as a writer, as possible.

This, then, is the story of how a group of radical young gay men and lesbian women met and supported the men, women and children of an isolated and rather traditional Welsh mining community; how their acts of friendship were paid back and how they helped change life in Britain. It is told, almost exclusively, in their voices, just as they told it to me: I am simply proud to have written down their words and privileged to have been trusted with their life stories.

Now it's your turn to meet them.

CHAPTER ONE
MEET THE CAST – LGSM

MIKE JACKSON

I was born in Accrington, in Lancashire in 1954. It was one of those communities where there was an extended family like this on every street. But it was a filthy town, completely industrial and almost a hundred per cent working class. Many of the old houses were made out of millstone grit, which is absorbent, so they were literally black. And the sky was this relentless grey – you only get sixty days of sunshine a year in Accrington – with constant drizzle. I remember that, when colour television was announced, I didn't quite get it, 'cause I'd never really seen colour. Beige was a bit racy.

I had quite a happy childhood but in 1962 my dad was killed in a car crash. And from being a working-class family that was doing rather well economically, we kind of tumbled down the snakes-and-ladders board.

I passed my 11-plus and was sent to a boarding school. It wasn't a public school but it was a state grammar school. My mother suggested this because she thought I was being brought up in too feminine an environment: her, my aunt, my grandmother – all of whom were strong matriarchs, who I naturally looked up to. She must have been a bit naïve to think that sending me to a single-sex boarding school would cure my nascent homosexuality.

I was bullied relentlessly at this school. I was the only working-class boarder and, being a little softie, I never fought back. I was petrified there. I remember walking along the banks of the river Ribble, looking longingly at the waters and thinking that would be release: suicide. Eventually, my mother withdrew me after a friend warned her that boarding schools were rife with homosexuality.

I absolutely doted on my grandma. When Winston Churchill died in 1965, I came home from school full of this kind of indoctrination about him, and my grandmother hit the roof. She hated him because – in her words – 'he set the troops on our own men.' She was referring to the coal miners: Churchill set the troops on miners twice – once in Tonypandy, in Wales, and once up in the north-east of England. She also used to tell me, 'Don't let them tell you they were the good old days. They weren't: they were rotten.'

So she was really the first person to teach me about politics. But it wasn't from an academic point of view: it was literally her life that she'd lived and she *hated* the Tories because of that. She used to tell me that, in the days before radio sets in their homes, during general elections people would go into Accrington town centre to stand outside the Town Hall and the Mayor would come out and read out the election results. She said that people would sit down and weep if the Tories got in because they knew they would be on a hiding. So Grandma really taught me my 'heart' politics. In my last year of school, when I was fifteen, I joined the Labour Party.

Because I wasn't very bright at school, I was in danger of ending up working in the huge factory in town. But I had always been interested in horticulture and, when I left school in 1970, I got a wonderful job working in the beautiful demonstration gardens in Worcester. So I left home at the same time as I left school. And two years later, when I was nineteen, I became a diploma student at Kew Gardens, which brought me to London.

BRETT HARAN

I was born in May 1959 in Oldham. It's an old cotton town: although it had once had coal mines, these were long closed by the time I grew up there. It was a very typical working-class background. I was the oldest of four boys and my early childhood was a bit fractured because my parents had something of a troubled relationship. My father was a bit of a 'Jack the lad' and often not around. He was nominally a painter and decorator but basically he was a labourer, who never really held down a job for any length of time. I once asked Mum what Dad's job was. She told me he was a 'fret worker': he worked for one week and fretted for the next three. He and Mum got married very young and we all came along in rapid succession: I think that Dad never really got to grips with the fact that he was a married man with kids.

Dad died when I was fourteen so my mum had to bring us up on her own. It was a bit of a struggle: not an unhappy childhood across the board but disjointed and sometimes a bit chaotic. Mum had to keep body and soul together and keep us all fed. The house we grew up in had leaks in the roof and the electricity was cut off on more than one occasion.

I would come home from school to find Mum cooking with a pan on a coal fire because the electric bill hadn't been paid. Eventually, when I was seventeen, Mum battered Oldham council into re-housing us in a brand-new council house with a downstairs and an upstairs toilet and central heating. We thought we'd died and gone to heaven.

Ours was a very traditional 'tribal Labour' household: all my family on both sides always voted Labour. Mum wasn't overtly political but, when it came to elections, she was rabidly anti-Tory. It wasn't anything deeper than that we knew we were Labour and that the Tories were the enemy.

I went to the local junior school and did well. I passed the entrance for Manchester Grammar School. From there I went on to Oxford University to study French and Russian. But my time at Oxford wasn't a happy one. I fell head over heels in love with a boy who was on the same course as me. Sadly, my feelings weren't reciprocated and, as a result, I couldn't wait to finish my degree and leave.

MARTIN GOODSELL

I was born in Fulham, west London, in 1959 and have lived in London all my life. I came from a working-class family: big families on both sides, all from around the west-London area. Both my mum and dad were the youngest of nine in their families. I grew up in a very close community because there were so many family members around. I was one of four kids.

My mum, before she was married, had worked in the rag trade, making swimming costumes. My dad was a labourer with a very low income but we had a lot of support from the extended family. So I grew up with a big family around me: a very close family – the sort of family that doesn't seem to exist these days. Our neighbours were considered to be part of the family and everybody knew everybody else's business.

I didn't come from a political family at all. They were Labour voters but on a lot of issues they were quite nationalistic, I suppose. My mum's sister married a man from Dominica in the Caribbean, so my cousins were black. The whole area where we lived was very cosmopolitan so I didn't quite get the whole racism thing. I mean, it was there – I knew it was there, even in my own family – but we all seemed to get on with each other very well.

I went to a local school, which was a bit notorious at the time. When I left school, I had the chance to go to university, but I'd fallen in love with a boy at school and we'd had a little thing going. When he decided to leave the sixth form, I was a bit forlorn and miserable. I was really lovesick and couldn't wait to leave school and so I went to work in the antiques trade.

RAY GOODSPEED

I was born in 1959, the youngest of six children, and brought up in the Kingston-upon-Thames area. When I was thirteen, we moved to Banbury in Oxfordshire. My dad was an unskilled factory worker and, when the factory re-located, we moved with his job.

A whole new council estate was built to accommodate all the people who had moved out of London. And so I found myself as a little working-class kid in this relatively working-class part of town.

My dad was a lifelong trade unionist. He was a building worker in the 1950s but he was blacklisted for union activities and so he had to get jobs in other industries, while mum worked in shops like Woolworth.

I was probably no more than twelve years old when I first felt I wasn't like other boys and wasn't having the same sexual dreams as them. So I looked up homosexuality in the index of my little *Pears' Cyclopaedia*, the book of knowledge (I've still got that edition of *Pears'*). It was listed under mental illnesses but it also said that I shouldn't worry because it was just a phase that many boys went through. So I went through years waiting to grow out of this phase.

I also remember watching a TV documentary around that time about one of the first gay-wedding-type ceremonies in America. It showed two men kissing: my dad started making retching noises and even I found it a bit much to watch. And in any TV drama, gay characters (where they existed) always had sad lives. They might be amusing for a while but they always had sad lives and then they just died.

14

No one in my family stayed on at school past the age of fifteen, much less went to university. I did: I went to Newcastle University to read English.

CLIVE BRADLEY

I was born in 1959. I grew up in Twickenham, west London. My family was middle class: my dad was a manager at a factory but his father had been a miner in County Durham. I had one older sister. My parents were both members of the Labour Party. My dad was quite a solid supporter of the mid-1970s Labour government and there would be lots of arguments in our house between him my sister's boyfriend, who was much more left wing.

NIGEL YOUNG

I was born in Hackney in 1946. I come from a very dysfunctional family. I've always been left wing: from a very early age I went on 'Ban the Bomb' demonstrations. But I didn't get my politics from my family, that's for sure.

I had failed my 11-plus and went to a secondary-modern school before going on to a college of further education. The head teacher thought that some of us should apply for university. I remember saying that I didn't know what university was. I just wanted to get away as far as possible from home as soon as I could. So I chose all these universities that were as far away as possible. But I couldn't get into any of them because I didn't have an O Level in a foreign language, which you needed in those days. But I re-applied and I found myself going to the

London School of Economics. I always think that I owed that to Harold Wilson because he opened up universities. He was quite important for all of our lives: perhaps if he'd known where we would all end up, he wouldn't have done that.

I wanted to read social anthropology but it was a very right-wing department and so I decided to do sociology instead. Right-wingers then thought that wasn't really a subject. I was at LSE from 1966–70: it was an incredibly lively time to go.

Everything was exciting as things were kicking off – student sit-ins and riots through all the glory years of LSE, anti-Vietnam demos, Grosvenor Square. I don't know that I understood it all really but I went on loads of demonstrations – anti-Rhodesia, those sorts of things. It was a time when you were expected to have ideals. There was even a point in time when I was a Maoist but I don't think that lasted very long.

I'd always wanted to be a teacher. So I eventually took a post-graduate course in education and in 1970 went to teach in a primary school in Hackney. I became a trade-union representative at the school where I taught. I worked there until around 1980 when I'd had enough – and at that point, sex, drugs and rock 'n' roll were playing a large part in my life.

JONATHAN BLAKE

I was born in Birmingham in 1949. I came from a traditional middle-class Jewish family: my mother's father was a Rabbi and he was Orthodox. My mother was born in Swansea, which is important to part of the story, but in 1914 she and her family emigrated from there to Winnipeg in Canada. In 1926 her father died, leaving them 'borassic' so they had to sell everything and come back to Britain.

My grandmother's sister had married a man called Louis Silkin and they lived in Dulwich so my mother and her family came back and lived with the Silkins. He was a lawyer and, by inclination, a Tory but in those days Jews couldn't join the Tory party so he joined the Labour Party. For some reason he was ennobled – he was given a baronetcy, a hereditary peerage, the full works.

My mother hated him. He had a mistress so, as far as she was concerned, he was the pits because her aunt was being cheated on. And so, for my mother, this tarred the whole Labour movement. Even though she was a natural socialist, she said she could never vote for the Labour Party. So I grew up in this conservative (with a small C) household in Birmingham.

My dad was in the house-furniture business. His family had obviously had money at some point because they lived in big houses and had servants but he was a shopkeeper basically, though with all the pretensions that had been given to him. He had been sent to a public school and he was determined that we should all go to one as well. So I went to Oundle public school.

I knew as a kid that I was homosexual: I was 'other'. So, for me, it was bliss: I was in a public school where there weren't any women, and boys were boys – they liked to have sex so that was the norm. That was fine by me – I was happy with all of that. But otherwise, I didn't enjoy school: I suppose I was part anarchist really. The only saving grace was that Oundle did plays.

My mother loved theatre and ballet and took me off to Stratford to see plays there. I remember turning to my mother and saying, 'I want to be an actor.' She replied, 'Well, I hope not like John Gielgud.' Gielgud had been caught 'cottaging' [soliciting for sex in a public toilet]. That went completely over my head at the time – but I remembered it later.

I left school in 1967 and went to drama school in Sidcup in Kent. This school also gave out teaching training certificates and this, for my parents, was the olive branch: I could always be a teacher if I failed as an actor. In 1972 I got a part on a BBC TV series, *The Regiment*, set in South Africa during the Boer war. The outside scenes – which were set in a concentration camp – were filmed near Neath in the South Wales valleys.

COLIN CLEWS

I was born in 1952 in a mining community in Ouston, County Durham in north-east England. I'm the youngest of three brothers. My family was traditional working class with a mining background. My grandfather was a mining hero. He rescued his mate when they were caught in a rock fall; his mate was completely buried and my grandfather dragged him free and pulled him to safety.

My father was the first man in the family not to work as a miner in the pit: when he first left school he went down the pit for two weeks then came home and begged his parents to let him find another job.

So he became a bus driver and then went on to be a minor civil servant at the Royal Ordnance factory. But we still lived in the pit village. I guess that's where I got my understanding of mining communities and the sense of community itself.

Ours wasn't a political family: quite the opposite. It was 'keep your head down' – a very traditional family with very traditional gender roles. So there were no politics in the family and no political awareness, beyond the fact that we lived in a mining village and so, when there was a strike and our neighbours were out on strike, my mum would go shopping and buy an extra packet of sausages or whatever to give to our neighbours to help them out.

But the message I grew up with was 'don't go down the pit. If you don't study, you will end up down the pit.' When I left school, it was a question of getting any job other than as a miner, so I became a civil servant, then a student psychiatric nurse and then in 1976 I went to Leicester Polytechnic as a mature student, studying English, history and politics.

DAVE LEWIS

I was born in Balham, south London in 1959. I moved to Tooting when I was eight. I had one half-sister who was nine years older than me. Dad was a milkman and Mum was an auxiliary nurse in a psychiatric hospital. My mother came from Ireland and my dad was born in Scotland but grew up in Newcastle.

We lived in a privately owned three-storey terraced slum. We all shared one room: there was a little kitchen area in the room and my dad put in a little partition wall to segment off a bit of the rest for my sister but I shared a bed with Mum and Dad. The toilet was down on the next floor and shared with the whole house.

There was no bathroom: we had a bath once a week on a Sunday night in a tin bath, which was hung up at the top of the stairs. I would get first dibs and my parents and my sister would go in after that. I grew up thinking that was absolutely normal; I thought everyone lived like this.

My family was tribally *Daily Mirror*-reading Labour. But if you pushed them on it – and I did when I was a teenager – they couldn't explain why.

I went to a Catholic primary school and then on to a Catholic grammar school four miles away from where I lived. All my friends went to the local comprehensive and I had to wear this poncey light-blue blazer with yellow trim. But I was never bullied: it helped that I was tall.

I was about thirteen when I began to suspect I was gay. I wasn't comfortable with this and I threw myself into religion for a couple of years. I was an altar boy at school and went on a couple of religious retreats. But it was sublimation really. I was uncomfortable about my sexuality and, at the same time, I developed sort of romantic-fantasy attachments with women: it was just like falling in love without ever telling them.

I went to Middlesex Polytechnic to do a philosophy, psychology and sociology degree. Within the first term, I realised that I was going to end up being a teacher or a social worker and I didn't want to be either. So I left and got a job at the Young Vic theatre, where I met some of the most fantastic, outrageous people. There I was one of only three people – out of a staff of forty – who claimed to be straight.

GETHIN ROBERTS

I was born in 1955 in North Wales and brought up first in Holyhead and then in Bethesda, a former slate-quarrying village where my mother's family came from. My father's father was a miner from South Wales and my other grandfather had been a quarryman. My father was a fireman and a trade unionist: he was a branch officer in the Fire Brigades Union (FBU). My mother was a teacher. They split up when I was five. I'm the middle of three brothers: all three of us are gay. When I was a teenager, we moved to Sevenoaks in Kent. My mother's father had died when she was very young so she was brought up by her mother, who was the youngest of seven children. All her sisters went into service but she was one of the first generation to go to University College North Wales, which had been funded largely by a voluntary levy that the quarrymen organized. She became a librarian.

When I was about nine, it began to dawn on me that I might be gay. My brothers and I all came out in chronological order, and my mother and grandmother, who with lived with us, were pretty accepting.

We weren't a particularly political family but my elder brother got involved in left-wing politics and I joined the Workers Revolutionary Party when I was fifteen. But two years later I'd grown up a bit and so I joined the Labour Party instead. Then in 1978 I went to Leeds University, as a mature student, to study sociology.

PAUL CANNING

I was born in 1962 in Rugby but grew up in Coalville in Leicestershire. I have one younger brother. At that time Coalville was still a mining town but it was also really a sort of exburb of Leicester. My dad was a pharmacist and had a little shop on a council estate. My parents were both from a working-class background so I was sort of lower middle class.

It wasn't really a political family. My father was a Conservative but he was a liberal Tory. I don't know about my mum. We didn't really do politics at home but I got interested from around the age of twelve. I can distinctly remember the 1974 election because Harold Wilson came to the Miners Welfare in Coalville and I slapped him on the back.

I knew I was gay at the age of sixteen and I came out to everybody then. I came out to my parents when we were on holiday and they kind of went a bit mad. The worst thing was that, when I came out at school – the local comprehensive – nobody said anything to me; there was, like, no effect at all. But years later I discovered that my brother had been bullied because of me, and that nobody had told me about it. To this day, my mother and my brother blame me for coming out.

I did go to a college – Huddersfield Polytechnic – to do economics but I wasn't really interested and, as soon as the opportunity presented itself, I moved to London.

STEPHANIE CHAMBERS

I was born in Nottingham in 1961. I don't have a father and I haven't spoken to my mother in twenty years. My mother was the black sheep of her family. She came from a military family who had real military minds. In the 1970s she came down to London to go on demonstrations and marches demanding equal pay for women. And she was one of those who were responsible for getting the law changed to get equal pay for women. But I wasn't a political person growing up. I felt politics didn't belong to me. It wasn't my world.

I first knew I was gay when I had sex in a haystack with my cousin's friend: I must have been about seven or eight. And from then on I knew I was gay and it wasn't an issue for me. My mother is a lesbian – though she didn't know that I was. When I was still very young, I managed to get into a gay nightclub in Nottingham. My mother came round the corner in the nightclub and I saw her: she didn't see me and I spent the rest of the night trying to dodge her. I'm not a lesbian because she is. It just happened that way. I did eventually tell her I was a lesbian and it turned out to be a problem. Not for the fact of my being gay but because she said I was copying her.

I qualified as a nurse in 1981 and came down to London and got a job in the National Hospital for Neurosurgery and Neurology. In those days you had to wear linen frocks and starched linen aprons and, as you got more senior, your starched hats got bigger. My family – such as it was – disowned me when I went to London because their attitude was that I was going there to take drugs.

WENDY CALDON

I was born in 1956 in Clerkenwell in central London. I'm from a working-class background. My dad was a driver for the *Evening Standard* – he used to deliver the papers – and my mum was a housewife.

They were both really hardworking. I think they'd both had a really tough time in the war – my dad was on the frontline in Africa, Italy and Greece, and Mum lived through the fire and bombs of the Blitz. It was tough on them but their attitude to life was that you should work to live, not live to work. Both my parents worked really hard to make us happy, though there wasn't a lot of money.

It was a very traditional working-class, cockney family. We lived in a council flat. I had two sisters, both quite a bit older than me. I was a bit of a runt, off sick from school a lot, but it was a very happy childhood. Both my parents were staunch old-guard Labour, both very much into trade unionism. My dad always used to say that, if you're working class and vote Tory, you're mad.

Education wasn't particularly important in my family, especially because we were all girls. My oldest sister was very bright and she went to grammar school. For a working-class girl at that time, going to grammar school was extraordinary. My dad used to say to us, 'You're a girl. You're going to get married. Don't worry about an education.'

I left school at sixteen. After working in a bank and then at a publisher, I got a job in the subs department at the *New Statesman* magazine. Later I joined Camden Council. I was so lucky: at that time it was a socialist council and it had money.

NICOLA FIELD

I was born in Buckinghamshire in 1960. My family was very 'home counties': Conservative, Tory-voting. It was a very nuclear family – I had one sister. But Mum and Dad split up in 1967, which was very unusual for ordinary people then and that had a huge effect on me. Emotionally, obviously, but also it created in me a sense of not belonging and of being different from that early stage in my life.

My town, High Wycombe, was incredibly Conservative but it was a divided population – socially and racially. It was two societies: Asian people who worked in factories lived on one side of town and all the white people lived on the other.

But this was also a time of huge social and political ferment and I was seeing things on the television that were telling me there was an alternative to the life I was living.

There were people protesting on the streets; students and feminists protesting – a whole world of ideas in which people were protesting at the way the world was. So I started kind of protesting against the way my family was and at the way I was being coerced and corralled into traditional gender roles and expectations.

I was first attracted to girls when I was fifteen. I was magnetised by a girl at my school and had a sexual dream about her. That really scared me. I was scared that I was a monster, abnormal, a freak: I was unspeakable.

PRIDE

I grew up listening to my transistor radio: cultural programmes, drama programmes on Radio 3 and Radio 4. When I went to university to read English, I never really went back home again.

CHAPTER TWO

MEET THE CAST – SOUTH WALES MINING FAMILIES

HYWEL FRANCIS

I was born in 1946 in the village of Onllwyn at the top end of the Dulais Valley. There were collieries all the way up and down the valley: between fifty and sixty thousand miners lived in our communities in South Wales when I was a boy.

I was the first of five generations of my family not to go down the pits. My mother was the daughter of a miner and trade unionist, and all her brothers were miners.

My father worked in Onllwyn Colliery and, eventually, was the general secretary of the South Wales Area of the National Union of Mineworkers, as well as the first chair of the Wales TUC. He lived through the first terrible period of post-war pit closures – ninety-one pits shut down in the 1960s – and also the Aberfan disaster, as well as horrible explosions in several mines. He was prominent during the two big miners' strikes of 1972 and 1974. So I was steeped in both trade unionism and politics. Like my father, I became a member of the Communist Party.

I went to university and developed a particular interest in history. I wrote the history of the Welsh miners who fought in the Spanish Civil War and the official history of the Welsh miners' union – the Fed. I founded the South Wales Miners' Library and I was involved in setting up the Coalfields Archive, which brought together all the records of the South Wales coalfields. And I ended up teaching history at Swansea University.

My father died in 1981, three years before the big strike. We don't forget our history here: there is a recognition that you are the bearer of that history, both in your family and in your community – and it marks you really.

DAI DONOVAN

I was born in Ynyswen in the Swansea Valley. My father was a miner and my uncles and grandparents all worked in the coal industry. There were four children – I was the eldest boy.

It wasn't a political home at all. My father was a hardworking, dedicated man but he never told us how to vote or anything like that. I don't think we even had a newspaper in the house. But we were brought up with a deep sense of responsibility and, although I didn't realise it, growing up, my bearings in life were socialist.

It was a time when society seemed more equal – or at least

there was the possibility to be what you wanted to be. But I was a dunce: I left school at fifteen with no qualifications and had a period of unemployment before joining the Royal Air Force for five and a half years. I joined because I had an interest in aircraft – and because I didn't want to go underground.

But then, after the RAF, I went into the coal industry – first in the washery and then underground at Abernant Colliery.

CHRISTINE POWELL

I was born in 1956 in Neath. I have one younger brother. We grew up in Seven Sisters, which is a village a little way up the Dulais Valley.

My mam was a nurse and my dad was a clerk in a colliery. He had started as a fitter, working underground, but gradually moved up to work in the office until he was forced out of mining and went to work for the Ford Motor Company factory. His elder brother worked underground for forty years, as did his brother-in-law. And my grandfathers both worked underground.

I think my dad's generation, in an area like this, was political without realising it. Everyone was brought up with the union.

When we were kids, there was a good community life here. There was a lot of community spirit and we looked after ourselves. There was a Boys Club, a cinema, cafés and a fantastic outdoor swimming pool, like a lido almost. Under the old miners' welfare system, all the men used to pay a little bit every week from their wages. But everything was supported by the men working underground and, as each colliery in turn was shut down, all those community things started to deteriorate and then close.

In 1975 I went to Cardiff University to read physics. I loved the subject and, since I'd wanted to be a teacher all my life, that's what I went into. I moved home to Seven Sisters and in 1980 married my husband, Stuart. He was an underground miner in Blaenant and his father before him had worked underground.

I was always political from when I was a teenager but I only joined the Labour Party after university: I thought student politics were like school. By 1981 I was a Labour councillor here in the village.

SÎAN JAMES

I was born in 1959 in the Swansea Valley, which is at next door to the Dulais Valley. I had one younger brother and there were just fourteen months between us so we were brought up very closely together.

I come from an entirely working-class family. My grandparents were in the mining and rail industries in the Upper Swansea Valley. It was a very traditional Welsh upbringing and Welsh was our first language. My father had worked in the coal mines during the war and, when the war ended and mining ceased to be a reserved occupation, he joined the RAF. However, because my mother wouldn't go into RAF accommodation with him, he came out of the RAF and got a job in a big watch factory. Many years later he went back to work in the colliery. My brother also went to work there but he hated every minute of it – absolutely hated it.

We weren't the sort of typical socially conservative family of the times. I grew up in a family where everybody expressed an opinion, and if you didn't, well, God help you. My parents were political in the sense that they were active voters and active trade unionists: my mother was an auxiliary nurse and a shop steward in NUPE, and my father was in the NUM. They believed that everybody should vote and they were always discussing politics – it was a massive subject in our family – always talking about current affairs, locally, nationally and internationally. My mother came from a family of five children, all politically active in the community but without any ambition to hold office. It was enough that you played your part.

Even more important than our strong trade unionism was a very, very strong Christian ethic. My parents weren't overly religious (I don't mean that they didn't believe) but we all went to church and chapel regularly. Their Christian ethic was that you always told the truth: never tell lies and shame the devil; you should never worry about telling the truth because the truth would always defend you. And you should always stand up for people who were less fortunate than yourself.

I went to a very big secondary-modern school but, even though there were 800 of us, everybody knew everybody. We were told every day that we were the worst of the worst: one teacher made us stand up and recite, 'We blocks, we stones, we worse than senseless things.'[1]

At my school all the girls did typing and cookery and

---

[1] In Shakespeare's *Julius Cesar*, the tribune (judge) Murullus calls the citizens of Rome 'you blocks, you stones, you worse than senseless things.'

sewing class, and the boys did woodwork. When I asked to do woodwork, I was told not to be a silly billy. Our sex education was something called 'health and hygiene' – which I'm still a bit baffled about. It consisted of copying out pages from books about sweat glands and athlete's foot while the teacher sat at the front of the class reading a novel.

I left school at sixteen, with five O Levels and a maths CSE, to get married. We lived with my parents for a year and then we got a house in a new development that must have been one of the last waves of local authority building houses for people. My abiding memory of living there was that there was nothing: not a post office nor a shop, not even a telephone box. But it was a community and I was active in getting some facilities for the families. I was always involved and always active: if there was something to be said – especially something unpleasant – I was the one who would say it. So I always had a reputation for saying what I thought.

JAYNE FRANCIS-HEADON

I was born in 1968 in Onllwyn, a village near the top of the Dulais Valley. Legally, I am the daughter of Hefina Headon, who was a formidable woman, the heartbeat of our community and one of the most important figures in the whole story. My birth mother was Hefina's daughter and, therefore, Hefina was actually my grandmother. But she and her husband, John, formally adopted me and I was raised as their daughter: I always called Hefina my mam.

When I was eight, we moved to Seven Sisters, which is the

village next to Onllwyn. By that time there wasn't a working pit in Onllwyn anymore. There was just the washery, which is where the coal was taken to be washed. The nearest pit was at Blaenant Colliery, which was where my father and my brother-in-law both worked underground. Most people in the villages around us worked at Blaenant: this was very much a mining community.

We were all just one big family: everybody knew everybody else and everybody looked out for one another. Mining was the main employer for all the people in these villages – all the men worked in the pit or in the washery, and women worked in ancillary jobs like the canteens at the collieries. It was almost all coal-industry related.

It seemed then like everyone had pretty much the same amount of money – and that was not a lot. It was a hand-to-mouth existence. Nobody went on foreign holidays; we didn't have that extravagant kind of lifestyle. It was always in a caravan or the beach for a day: there wasn't any of that extravagant kind of living. It was very working class.

Our house was a council house: most of the villagers lived in council houses. Some had originally been Coal Board houses but by the 1970s they had been taken over by the council.

Growing up, the community did feel quite insular to me. Our exposure to life outside the village was very minimal. We had a phone but not everyone in the village did. We had a television, of course, but there wasn't really much on – it didn't start till 11am, did it? And Onllwyn is very small: there are only two streets in the village itself. When you stand in the villages of Onllwyn and Seven Sisters and you look around you, there's a mountain everywhere you look so you don't see beyond that. And so you do feel very insular in that community. You did feel, however, that you were embraced by Wales and the land.

I went to the Welsh school in the next-door valley – the Swansea Valley – over the mountain, as we used to say. There were only seven children in my year, and the year above only had three: it was very small. Everything was taught in Welsh – history was Welsh history and, though they told us there were other countries, it was also a case of 'this is all we care about and all that we're telling you about.'

My family was always staunch Labour. My mum was on the Labour Party committee and, during elections, she gave us children leaflets to deliver and we campaigned with her. She was definitely a socialist – she wanted life to be fair and for there to be something for everybody in the community, and that's what she fought for all her life.

CHAPTER THREE
A LITTLE HISTORY

On 1 January 1947, thousands of miners and their families across Britain marched to their local pit. The processions were led by colliery bands and the cheering families proudly carried union banners. When the marchers reached the mines, they crowded round newly installed plaques, which proclaimed, 'This colliery is now managed by the National Coal Board on behalf of the people'.

That New Year's Day marked the beginning of Britain's nationalised coal industry. The Act of Parliament that created it charged the National Coal Board (NCB) with providing Britain with adequate supplies of fuel whose quantity and price were to be predicated by the public interest. For miners who had lived and worked through the darkest days of privately owned pits – poor safety and fatal accidents, low wages and arbitrary lay-offs – the belief that coal would, henceforth, be mined for the common good was welcomed as the dawn of a new and enlightened era.

And so, for a few years, it was. A long fought-for five-day week was introduced and investment was made in new pits, while new safety laws and organised training reduced the potential for loss of life. Wages, too, rose steadily: by 1950 miners were at the top of the league table of industrial wages and were recognised as the aristocracy of manual labour.

———

HYWEL FRANCIS

In the 1950s I believed that the coal industry would go on forever. From the outset, coal nationalisation had been intended to ensure that any changes needed in the industry would be made by consent; that the ruthless management and lack of consultation which characterised the pre-1947 situation had been buried along with the old coal owners.

Then in the 1960s a programme of pit closures began. Those closures were economic: the more difficult seams were expensive to mine and, with imported oil being so cheap then, the generation of electricity began to move that way. And pits began to close all around us and there was a sense of there being no future for coal.

CHRISTINE POWELL

My dad worked first in Banwen Colliery until that closed in the 1960s. He moved to Seven Sisters Colliery and was told that would be the place to see him through his working life.

Shortly after, Seven Sisters closed. He then went down to Brynteg Colliery and that closed shortly after he got there. He then moved to the original Blaenant Colliery in the village of Crynant but later, just to get work, he had to go over to the Maesteg in the Llynfi Valley. It was very difficult for him to get there: he used to have to get up at a ridiculous time in the morning and wouldn't get home till very, very late. So in the end, he was forced out of mining and went to work for the Ford Motor Company.

———

In the same period, another group of people was experiencing the first rays of hope after years of persecution. From 1945–55 the number of prosecutions for homosexual behaviour rose from 800 a year to 2,500. By 1955 a third of those convicted were sent to prison, sometimes for up to two years. The increase in prosecutions was a direct result of government policy. The Director of Public Prosecutions, Sir Theobald Mathew, had been alarmed by a surge in homosexual activity during the war years: from 1944–64 he made the suppression of homosexuality a primary goal for police forces. Specific targets were set for arrests and the Metropolitan Police established training courses, preparing officers to go 'underground' and entrap gay men in known homosexual settings.

———

MIKE JACKSON

I had known from very early on in my childhood that I was gay but there wasn't much of a liberal culture in Accrington: in some ways, life there was pretty rough and brutal. So I absorbed all the homophobic messages around me: homosexuals were mad, they were dangerous, they were bad. And I completely internalised everything.

———

In 1957 the government-appointed Wolfenden Committee recommended that homosexual acts in private between two consenting adults should be decriminalised. 'Adults' – in the context of homosexuality – were defined as being over the age of twenty-one: the heterosexual age of consent was then sixteen.

The Committee also made clear that it regarded homosexuality as a debilitating condition, which should be treated, if possible, by medical means. Even these limited proposals would not be voted on in Parliament for another ten years. In the meantime, a movement began to demand repeal of anti-gay laws. And miners played a central – if largely unwitting – role.

———

MIKE JACKSON

The beginnings of gay liberation – the campaign to reform the law which made homosexuality illegal – started in the north-west of England.

Allan Horsfall was an out, working-class man who lived in a mining community. He lobbied all the trades unions, and especially the NUM, to support reform. He wrote a letter to the *New Statesman*, which was published, in which he said that he didn't understand why the national leadership of the NUM was being so timorous on this issue, because everyone accepted him in his community.

38

ALLAN HORSFALL

I was working for the National Coal Board at that time, and living in a house that belonged to the coal board in the middle of Atherton, a mining village in the south-Lancashire coalfield. I got our North-Western Homosexual Law Reform Committee notepaper printed with my address and we launched our first leaflet – 10,000 copies – and sent it to social workers, gay groups and to the press, of course. The local paper ran a front-page feature with a banner headline and I thought all hell was going to break loose.

Dennis Skinner, Labour MP for Bolsolver, wrote in the *New Statesman*, 'Well, yes, reform might be very admirable, but no way will it go down in my constituency with the miners.' So I replied, saying, 'Well, I'm publishing from the middle of a mining village, and I find it all right. I don't know what Skinner's on about.'[2]

———

In July 1967 a new Sexual Offences Act decriminalised homosexual acts between two men, above the age of twenty-one, provided these took place in private. After an intense all-night debate in the House of Commons, the legislation received Royal Assent on 27 July 1967. The Bill's sponsor, Arthur Gore, 8th Earl of Arran, took to the floor of the House of Lords to warn gay men that they were, effectively, on probation.

'I ask those [homosexuals] to show their thanks by comporting themselves quietly and with dignity ... any form of ostentatious

---

[2] Quoted in 'The Long March', the *Guardian*, 29 September 2004.

behaviour now or in the future or any form of public flaunting would be utterly distasteful … [And] make the sponsors of this Bill regret that they had done what they had done.'

The new law applied only in England and Wales, and it specifically exempted all members of the armed forces. It also made homosexual acts involving more than two adult males subject to prison sentences of up to two years. Because of the narrow definition of 'a public place', commercial bars and clubs catering to gay men risked police harassment.

––––

JONATHAN BLAKE

The law stated that only consenting adult males *in private* could have any sort of sexual contact. On Henrietta Street there was a gay club, which had bouncers, and, if two men were dancing together, these bouncers would prise you apart because it was illegal since there were more than two people in the property. As a result, people had house parties. But if you shared a flat and you brought someone home with you, the police could come and break down your door because there were more than two people in the property. And they did.

––––

These restrictions led many gay men to 'cruise' for sex in cemeteries and public toilets, known as 'cottages'. Police deployed young and attractive officers – so-called 'pretty police' – to entrap 'cottagers'.

––––

JONATHAN BLAKE

I was once in West Brompton cemetery and a 'pretty policeman' nabbed me and I was arrested. I wasn't sent to prison but I was taken to court, convicted and fined. And I thought, 'This is ridiculous: he came on to me, I didn't come on to him.' But that was the way it was – a constant threat.

NIGEL YOUNG

I was at LSE in 1967, the year homosexuality was legalised. The year before I was arrested for cottaging. It was all a bit stupid, I suppose, but one just gets carried away and doesn't take any notice of the signals that are around.

I was charged and tried and sent to prison for a week. I went to Brixton. That was hell – it was a hell. A week may not seem a long time but, as a young man, it was endless; monstrous.

JONATHAN BLAKE

There was continual harassment. Low-level for the most part, which every so often would flare up whenever the police's [arrest] quotas weren't high enough or someone decided 'let's go and bash some queers'. So there was always this threat that you lived with. Underneath it all, you were second class and you were 'other' and you could be attacked. And people were.

———

Between 1957 and 1964, 264 collieries closed – nearly one third of the pits which had been nationalised. The number of miners was reduced in almost equal proportion, while their wages fell steadily until they were no longer close to keeping up with inflation. The closures and erosion of pay caused a handful of short-lived local stoppages. But a combination of carefully managed (and sometimes generous) redundancy terms, coupled with a largely right-wing leadership of the National Union of Miners (NUM), ensured that these never developed into a national strike.

––––

DAI DONOVAN

The South Wales miners tried to challenge pit closures: there had been a number of sit-ins but we had failed to get the rest of the coalfields in England to support us.

––––

Then, in 1972, the NUM demanded substantial pay rises: Edward Heath's Conservative government rejected the claim and, on 9 January 1972, the first national pit strike for almost fifty years began.

––––

CHRISTINE POWELL

I remember the 1972 strike, sitting my mock O Levels in the school canteen because that was the only room that was heated by gas and there was no coal for the school boiler.

––––

The strike lasted six weeks and ended in victory for the NUM. It also brought new, more militant leaders to power inside the union: one was a young Yorkshire miner called Arthur Scargill.

By the end of 1973 international oil prices had risen dramatically and inflation had eroded much of the increases in miners' wages. NUM members began a work to rule aimed at reducing coal stocks at power stations and forcing the government to concede their pay claim.

HYWEL FRANCIS

In 1973 the oil price tripled. The economic power of the miners was temporarily much greater and coal was then very definitely seen as a key component of energy policy. The reality was that the miners were united at that time – and in very difficult circumstances.

———

On 1 January 1974 Heath's government introduced a three-day week for industry to preserve coal stocks by reducing demand for electricity.

———

CHRISTINE POWELL

The same thing happened for my mock A Levels as had happened for my mock O Levels: I sat them in the canteen because it had a gas fire and there was no coal to power the boiler which served the rest of the school.

———

On 5 February 1974 the NUM began a national strike. Two days later, with electricity restrictions and power cuts hitting homes as well as industry, Edward Heath called a general election. On 7 February he made a television appeal to the nation, asking, 'Who governs Britain?'

Prime Minister Edward Heath's Broadcast Appeal

Do you want a strong government which has clear authority

for the future to take decisions which will be needed? Do you want Parliament and the elected government to continue to fight strenuously against inflation? Or do you want them to abandon the struggle against rising prices under pressure from one particularly powerful group of workers?

This time of strife has got to stop. Only you can stop it. It's time for you to speak – with your vote.

It's time for your voice to be heard – the voice of the moderate and reasonable people of Britain: the voice of the majority. It's time for you to say to the extremists, the militants, and the plain and simply misguided: we've had enough. There's a lot to be done. For heaven's sake, let's get on with it.

———

HYWEL FRANCIS

When Edward Heath went to the country, he challenged the miners and asked the question 'Who rules this country? Is it us, the elected government, or is it you, a quarter of a million miners – an unelected minority of the population?' It was a very foolish thing to do. It was not the intention of the miners to bring down the government; it was just to get an improvement in their wages and conditions.

SÎAN JAMES

My dad went out in the coal strikes of 1972 and 1974. I remember going with my father to picket in Somerset. Not every kid went with their fathers then but my dad took me.

And here in South Wales it was always one out, all out. We'd always understood what the union was; understood the need to stick together and take collective action.

JAYNE FRANCIS-HEADON

I was six when the strike started but I have some memories of the three-day week. As well as being a miner, my father drove the village mini-bus and I can remember that he was more available, so to speak, at that time.

And I remember that we had to be quite spare with the heating and what we ate at the time. There were a lot of power cuts and so we had candles everywhere but the whole village was very tight in the strike – very together.

RAY GOODSPEED

I was already a leftie by the time I was a teenager. During the strike, I remember running round my school turning all the lights on, in every classroom, deliberately to burn as much electricity as possible to help the miners' cause. During the three-day week, I remember doing my homework by candlelight: whenever there was a blackout, other people would complain but me and my mum and dad cheered every time the lights went out.

———

Heath's demand that the electorate decide who ran Britain backfired. The Conservatives narrowly lost power in the February election and did so again in a second general election held in October. Harold Wilson's Labour government agreed a long-term strategy with the miners, which put a modernised and well-supported coal industry at the heart of the nation's industrial plans. For the first time in decades, investment was poured in and new coalfields were opened across Britain.

But Heath's defeat had another, and even more far-reaching, impact. The Conservative Party replaced him with a new leader.

CHAPTER FOUR
T.I.N.A.[3]

On 11 February 1975 Margaret Thatcher became leader of the Conservative Party. She had been Education Secretary in the Heath governments of 1970–74 and had imposed extensive cuts in the funding of state education. One of these – the abolition of free school milk for children aged seven to eleven – earned her the nickname 'Margaret Thatcher, Milk Snatcher'. As Leader of the Opposition, Mrs Thatcher abandoned the traditional Conservative Party 'One Nation' approach, advocating instead the shrinking of the welfare state, lower taxes and greater freedom for private enterprise. This ideological commitment to the free market involved reducing government support for nationalised industries and confronting the unions

---

[3] Throughout her premiership, critics derisively referred to Margaret Thatcher as 'Tina': this was an acronym, derived from her repeated use of the phrase 'There Is No Alternative'.

who supported it. The defeat inflicted on Heath by the NUM was uppermost in her thinking.

————

HYWEL FRANCIS

After the 1974 strike, the Tories began preparing and changing. Thatcherism was a new kind of Conservatism: it was much *harder* politics. They put together a secret report, which prepared for the eventuality of a big miners' strike and set out a plan to ensure that a Tory government would be able to win and to break the union stranglehold.

————

In June 1977 a confidential internal memorandum – The National Industries Policy Group Report – was distributed among Conservative Party leaders. The document, drawn up by right-wing MP Nicholas Ridley, put forward a draft plan for a future government to fight – and defeat – a major strike in a nationalised industry.

Nicholas Ridley: 'The Ridley Plan'

'More and more the nationalised industries are run for the benefit of those who work in them. The pressures are for jobs for the boys, and more money for each boy … it must eventually be taken for granted that … plants must be closed and people must be sacked.'

Ridley anticipated that the major public-sector unions – and especially the NUM – would fiercely resist his plans. To defeat the miners, he proposed building up coal stocks at power stations, importing supplies, training a large squad of mobile riot police to defeat picketing, and cutting off welfare benefits to strikers and their families. His report was adopted by Thatcher and her shadow cabinet and leaked to the right-wing *Economist* magazine in May 1978.

———

DAI DONOVAN

I knew immediately that Thatcher was going to be very dangerous. I felt intensely frustrated and I joined the Labour Party. I don't think I had any particular foresight: I thought she would come after us – the working class movement – but even then I didn't think she was going to come after the miners in particular.

———

Despite the (limited) decriminalisation of homosexuality a decade earlier, in the mid-1970s gay men and women were still experiencing discrimination, persecution and abuse.

———

JONATHAN BLAKE

The attitude of the police was horrible. We were just filth. Outside the Coleherne gay pub on a hot night there always used to be a police presence. In the long hot summer of 1976 there were riots in Earls Court because the police had been harassing gay men so much: there was continual harassment.

You'd also – on a regular basis – get verbal abuse from people in the street. People – young lads, mostly – would scream 'fucking queer' at you. It was always there in the air: an atmosphere of homophobia and menace.

The fact that I have any self-esteem is pretty amazing when you think of the weight of society against us. But I did feel then that people should come out openly if they were gay.

————

MIKE JACKSON

I twice went to my GP to see if I could get a cure for my homosexuality. But, fortunately, because I was so paranoid, when I went into the consulting room, I just told the doctor I had a cold. And thank God I did. In those days the doctor would probably have sent me for electroconvulsive therapy (ECT).

Within a few months of getting to London I had begun to read the classified [contact] ads in *Time Out*. But I was so paranoid about my sexuality that, when I read *Time Out* on the tube, I would constantly worry that the passengers on either side of me could see what I was looking at and would jump up and shout, 'Ha ha – you're a homosexual!'

I'd also read the advert for Gay Switchboard [telephone helpline] – many, many times. Eventually, I decided to ring them up but I had to go and find an isolated telephone box so none of my colleagues at Kew Gardens would walk past and see that I was phoning a homosexual telephone helpline. These poor volunteers would try to reassure me but I think I must have told them, 'I know you don't think there's anything wrong with it but I do!'

————

On 11 July 1977 the nationally distributed newspaper *Gay News* and its editor, Denis Lemon, were found guilty of blasphemous libel for publishing a poem by James Kirkup, which characterised

Jesus Christ as a homosexual. Both were fined and Lemon was given a suspended nine-month prison sentence. The case was brought by conservative moral reformer Mary Whitehouse but the law was archaic and her private prosecution required approval by government legal officers. In a sign of the prevailing antipathy towards homosexuality, this had been granted.

———

CLIVE BRADLEY

I remember being with my parents and watching an episode of the BBC police series *Softly Softly* in which there was a homosexual storyline: my mum turned to me and said, 'Doesn't it make you sick?' And that was the climate then; that's what was in the air.

DAVE LEWIS

The prevailing attitude was very negative. I lived on quite a big council estate in Tooting and one thing you didn't want to be known as was a sissy. And I was a sissy – gay and effeminate through and through – but I hid it, for self-preservation. And as a teenager, I joined in with the anti-gay stuff, because you had to. If my friends were saying about someone else, 'Oh, he's a queer,' I'd go, 'Yeah, yeah, I think you're right.' Which was incredibly damaging to myself.

MARTIN GOODSELL

There was general homophobia on the TV, which would be dished out by people you mixed with: calling someone 'queer' or a 'poof' was the biggest insult when I was growing up.

DAVE LEWIS

I remember watching Tom Robinson singing 'Glad to Be Gay' on TV in 1978. My parents were in the room and there was just complete silence. I didn't say anything and neither did they.

I was really pleased to see it, and it was the first image that I'd seen of someone who was gay and who said, 'Yeah – what about it?' All of the other images were of victims really: Larry Grayson, John Inman, Kenneth Williams.

NICOLA FIELD

It was a very homophobic atmosphere and gay people were seen as weirdos and freaks by my family, my teachers and the school. That homophobia was absolutely overt: gay people were called 'lezzies' and 'poofs'. A lesbian was seen as someone who was repulsive, had developed wrongly and would end up lonely and isolated. It was terrifying. I was quite religious as a teenager and I thought I would go to hell because of my sexuality. I felt that, if anyone ever found out the truth about me, I would be damned, doomed and lost.

GETHIN ROBERTS

In 1976 my older brother was involved with Bangor University Gay Society. It was investigated by the vice squad, who were seriously looking at the possibility of charging Gay Soc members with conspiracy to corrupt minors and public morals. There was a very large-scale police operation, including people being followed around by police helicopters.

At Leeds, I helped set up Leeds Gay Switchboard on university property. But we had to do it under the guise of running a science-fiction library. As far as the university authorities were concerned, we were running a sci-fi library.

More seriously, I also campaigned to defend gay students. In particular, a fellow student who had graduated applied to do a teaching conversion course. One of the requirements was a health certificate from his doctor at the university health service but the doctor refused to give him this on the grounds that he was gay.

MARTIN GOODSELL

There were raids on clubs by the police because, even in gay venues, men weren't allowed to dance together because there was a nineteenth-century by-law which prohibited 'licentious dancing'. That simply meant two men dancing – quite normally – together. If people danced together in the Coleherne, for example, the staff would come up and tell them to stop.

There was also entrapment in toilets – and even outside clubs – by 'pretty police'. I read the local paper and every single week – without fail – you would see court reports, naming people and giving their address, saying they had been prosecuted for 'importuning', either at Brompton Cemetery or in an alleyway somewhere. It was quite scary knowing that the police were doing this, actively seeking people out.

COLIN CLEWS

You can get a sense of the climate by what happened to the editor of *Gay News*, Dennis Lemon. [He] was arrested for photographing police officers who were harassing customers at a London gay pub: he was held on suspicion of having stolen the camera!

JONATHAN BLAKE

As well as that, what you would also get was 'queer-bashing'. On Clapham Common and places like that there always the potential for that. There was always this underlying sense of threat and fear so that you could never completely relax. It does amaze me – given that I was out on the scene and not necessarily being as sensible or as covert as I might have been – that I was never actually queer-bashed. But I know people that were.

GETHIN ROBERTS

I got physically attacked at a student union event: I was wearing a gay badge and another student punched me – physically punched me – for being gay. I punched him back and knocked him out.

Then in London I was queer-bashed a few times. In one of the attacks, someone ran up, punched me in the face and left me with bits of blood and bone hanging out of my nose. There was a feeling of living under threat. I lived in a gay housing co-op and our houses all had screens to prevent firebombs because we had been threatened with that.

I never reported any of the attacks to the police: it wouldn't even have occurred to me to do so. The police were definitely homophobic and I knew I wouldn't have been taken seriously. The police harassed us: on the 1979 Gay Pride march in London, somebody was arrested for possessing an offensive weapon. It was, in fact, a *papier maché* prop – it was part of his headdress. So we all sat down in the middle of Oxford Street and refused to move. People then got arrested for that.

————

Between November 1978 and February 1979, a seemingly endless financial crisis caused a succession of strikes by public-sector unions over pay. Newspapers coined the phrase 'the winter of discontent'. On 28 March 1979 Labour Prime Minister James Callaghan lost a vote of confidence in the House of Commons and announced plans for a general election. The Conservative Party manifesto gave no clue as to Mrs Thatcher's radical plans to restructure Britain's economy.

Conservative Party 1979 Election Manifesto

'A strong and responsible trade union movement can play a big part in our economic recovery … We believe that a competitive and efficient coal industry has an important role in meeting energy demand…'

On 3 May 1979 the Conservative Party won the general election. The following day television cameras filmed Margaret Thatcher speaking on the front step of 10 Downing Street:

'I know full well the responsibilities that await me as I enter the door of No. 10 and I'll strive unceasingly to try to fulfil the trust and confidence that the British people have placed in me and the things in which I believe.

And I would just like to remember some words of St Francis of Assisi, which I think are really just particularly apt at the moment. 'Where there is discord, may we bring harmony. Where there is error, may we bring truth. Where there is doubt, may we bring faith. And where there is despair, may we bring hope.'

————

MIKE JACKSON

She'd come into power like this screaming witch; this banshee. Everything she stood for was anathema – to me and to millions of other people. And when she got into Number Ten and stood on the doorstep quoting St Francis of Assisi, my jaw dropped. It was such a potent moment. What a hideous, hideous idea that someone like her would quote those wonderful words about bringing harmony. 'No, you won't,' I thought. 'No you won't.'

GETHIN ROBERTS

I remember feeling absolute horror and gloom the day after the 1979 election. It was really distressing. Thatcher was already known as 'The Milk Snatcher' – so we all knew the kind of person she was: she had that kind of history of nastiness from being in the Heath government.

She was already perceived to be strident and uncompromising. But nobody truly realised what she was planning: I didn't wake up on that morning thinking, 'Oh, now she's going to go after the miners.' But I think I realised that she would want revenge for 1973 and 1974.

MARTIN GOODSELL

I knew instinctively something bad was going to happen. Everything about the woman was wrong. Alarm bells were going off in my mind because everything she was about was taking us back to the 1950s. And all the free-market economics behind her policies: I knew that she was a really serious threat; a serious enemy.

SÎAN JAMES

We knew what it was going to mean once she was elected. I talked with other young families and we all realised that things were going to be very different from then on. And my dad told me that she would be out to get the miners – he knew she was going to come after them. Everyone had a sense of impending doom: we knew that we were facing a very repressive Conservative government.

HYWEL FRANCIS

In the week that Thatcher won that 1979 general election, I took a group of Welsh miners out to America on a visit. There was a revolution in coal production going on there, moving away from unionised mines into non-union pits. We were asked who this woman was now running our country. I remember saying, 'We know nothing much about her at all – but she won't last.'

And when we saw the conditions of the miners in America – attacks on wages, pit closures, scab unions and private, not public, ownership of mining – that week, we thought we were looking at our past. But unbeknown to us, we were actually looking at our future. That was what was going to befall us.

CHAPTER FIVE

BATTLE LINES

During the general election, the Conservatives had deployed a widespread poster campaign showing a photograph of a long dole queue and the slogan 'Labour Isn't Working'. When Mrs Thatcher assumed office, a record 1.1 million people were unemployed. But she was committed to a radical economic theory – monetarism – which demanded that controlling inflation (then running at 10 per cent) was the government's overriding priority. To achieve this goal – while simultaneously lowering taxes for high earners and boosting the defence budget – the government imposed tough cuts in public spending.

———

SÎAN JAMES

And very, very quickly there were job losses. There was no opportunity, there were no apprenticeships, just Mickey

59

Mouse YTS job-training schemes where young people learned nothing.

RAY GOODSPEED

I graduated in 1980 and it was impossible to get a job in Newcastle. Thatcher had destroyed the city: everything closed down – steel, the shipyards. It was in ruins economically. Newcastle was a wasteland, with gangs of men who used to work and gangs of boys who would probably never work.

———

In January 1980 workers in the nationalised British Steel Corporation (BSC) began a national strike over pay. The dispute lasted fourteen weeks and secondary picketing spread to private steelmakers and the country's dockyards. The strike ended with what appeared, at first, to have been a victory for the union. But within months, the government installed a new and aggressive chairman at the BSC. Ian McGregor had a reputation as a cost-cutter at any price: within months 17,000 of the 24,000 steelworkers in South Wales were put on short time. The same year, a new Employment Act imposed restrictions on secondary picketing and the economic outlook continued to worsen. By the middle of 1980 the number of people unemployed was approaching two million and the Prime Minister faced repeated calls to change her policy. At the 1980 Conservative Party conference, she uttered the immortal words:

Margaret Thatcher: Conservative Party Conference, October 1980

'To those waiting with bated breath for that favourite media catchphrase, the U-turn, I have only one thing to say: You turn if you want to. The lady's not for turning.'

Despite the government's tough monetarist policies, inflation was rising steadily, peaking at more than 20 per cent. By the end of the year Mrs Thatcher's job approval rating fell to 23 per cent – lower than recorded for any previous prime minister.

————

CLIVE BRADLEY

In her first year in power I remember being surprised: I had expected much more resistance – much more organised resistance – to her. But it just didn't happen.

There was a steel strike – which she had effectively won – and I'd begun to feel a kind of disappointment that she was able to do what she did; that Thatcher was much more solidly in power than I'd thought would be possible.

————

At the end of 1980 the NUM was the most powerful union in the country – and the one most firmly in the government's sights. But Mrs Thatcher was not yet ready to take on the miners.

————

SÎAN JAMES

In the early days, we in the mining valleys were a bit cushioned. My daughter was born just after Thatcher was elected and I can remember my father telling my husband, Martin, 'Go and work underground. That'll be a job for life – we'll always need coal in this country.' And Martin did: he went back to the mines because that's what we believed – we were sure that there would always be mining. Of course, this was at the time that world markets were being opened up: we hadn't foreseen that, to get hard currency, the Soviet Union would dump cheap coal on us and that the price on the dockside would drop dramatically.

———

In January 1981 the government told the NCB that it was cutting back the funding which subsidised the industry. The decision forced the board to propose the closure of twenty-three pits.

———

HYWEL FRANCIS

When the NCB announced its plans, spontaneous strikes broke out in South Wales and these were followed by actions in other coalfields across the country. These led the government to back down and withdraw the threats of closure – at least for the time being.

CHRISTINE POWELL

In 1981 we had barely been married a year when my husband, Stuart, went out on strike for a fortnight. But it was plain that Thatcher wasn't quite ready for the miners at this point, so she appeased them.

———

But the government's retreat was no more than a tactic to buy time. Mrs Thatcher began preparing for a full and final future confrontation with the miners. The first step was to hamstring the union movement – already weakened by mass job losses – with new laws. The 1980 Employment Act restricted secondary picketing and imposed a maximum limit of six people on any picket line. Meanwhile, the miners were also preparing for a fight. In 1981 the NUM replaced its outgoing right-leaning President, Joe Gormley, with the fiery Yorkshire left-winger Arthur Scargill. He won overwhelming support from across the coalfields.

SÎAN JAMES

My father was a huge supporter of Arthur Scargill. I remember in 1981 my dad saying, 'I'm going to hear this guy speak. You've got to come and hear him speak with me – he is the future of the union.'

He – and all of us – were tired of the way the union had been run by the previous leaders. And he knew there were big battles coming.

HYWEL FRANCIS

In the early 1980s Yorkshire had the most miners – 60,000 compared with around 20,000 in Wales. South Wales supported Yorkshire Area NUM leader Arthur Scargill as President of the NUM because they felt they could trust him to mobilise Yorkshire – and, with it, the rest of the British coalfields. Everybody knew that a successful strike wouldn't be possible without the Yorkshire miners' support.

In April 1981 the recession caused by the government's economic policies was hitting hard. Unemployment rose to 2.5 million and, amid increasing hostility between communities and the police, riots broke out across Britain. They began in the deprived inner-city area of Brixton, South London on 10 April. For forty-eight hours up to five thousand people fought pitched battles with the police.

———

NIGEL YOUNG

I was living in Brixton during the riots. I was squatting further down the road from where I live now. I hated Thatcher. I could see from the outset what she was about. But on one of the two nights, I was faced with a dilemma. I'd got tickets for Janet Baker in *Julius Caesar* at the Coliseum – and I loved Janet Baker – on the same day as the riots were going on. I had to make a decision: do I join the riots or do I go to the opera? Do I throw petrol bombs at the police or go to the Coliseum?

In the end, I climbed over the barricades to go to see Janet Baker – which actually saved me: some of my friends were jailed.

———

Throughout 1981 opinion polls showed Mrs Thatcher to be a deeply unpopular leader. In March 364 economists signed a letter, published in *The Times,* calling for a change in government policy. It was ignored and, by the end of the year, unemployment reached 3 million – 12.5 per cent of the workforce – a level not seen for 50 years. It seemed certain that Mrs Thatcher would be a one-term Prime Minister. But, in February 1982, Argentina invaded the Falkland Islands. Mrs Thatcher's reaction was to send a military task force to the south Atlantic and the country found itself at war.

———

SÎAN JAMES

The Falklands War was the big turning point for us – especially in this part of Wales. More than a hundred years before, a group of people had left the valleys and gone to Patagonia in Argentina, where they set up a Welsh-speaking community. That community thrived and, when the war happened, we knew that some of the young soldiers fighting for Argentina would be called David Jones, or whatever: they might speak Welsh with a Spanish accent but they still spoke Welsh. So how could they be the enemy? On top of that, much of the Falklands was owned or managed by British coal companies – and we saw how they had always treated us here in the Welsh coal-mining communities. So we were very, very torn about the Falklands. We didn't understand why we were going to war.

DAI DONOVAN

I don't know that all miners shared my horror of Thatcher. I can remember one conversation underground on the night that one of the British ships was sunk: a colleague started talking about 'fucking Argies, sinking our ships'. My reaction was, 'What the fuck did you think they were going to do?' But they were readers of the *Sun* and all that came with that.

———

In June 1982 Argentine forces on the Falklands surrendered. The war had lasted two months, one week and five days. It had cost the lives of 255 British servicemen and 649 Argentinean soldiers, many of them young and unwilling conscripts. The war led to the fall of the Argentine military junta; it also reversed Mrs Thatcher's political fortunes and helped her to a landslide victory in the 1983 general election.

————

SÎAN JAMES

I'm not saying that Argentina didn't behave badly but we could see clearly that Thatcher wanted her Churchillian moment; she wanted a jingoistic war to give her a bounce in the polls – which she needed badly because she was so unpopular. And that's exactly what she got: she won an election off the back of it and we knew then there was another four or five years of her – so what was going to happen next? Did we realise she would come for us then? I'm not sure.

————

The war 'triumph' strengthened Mrs Thatcher's grip on power and heralded an increasing unease about the apparent militarisation of Britain.

As the US Air Force prepared to move nuclear-tipped Cruise missiles into an airbase at Greenham Common in Berkshire, hundreds of women – some feminists, some lesbians, some simply fearful for the future – set up a peace camp beside the road leading into the base.

————

SÎAN JAMES

I went to Greenham. There were women who lived there permanently and camps you could just join in as and when.

There were lesbian women there and I will have met them, but most of the women I was with were mothers, like me, and had a specific reason for being there – to protect our children and safeguard their future.

STEPHANIE CHAMBERS

I wasn't a political person growing up. I felt politics didn't belong to me. It wasn't my world. When I went to Greenham, it was primarily because that gave me an opportunity to meet women and be with women. They all seemed like intellectuals to me: they were strong women – Boadiceas.

SÎAN JAMES

We weren't very popular with the good people of Greenham and Newbury: the women couldn't go into local shops; they wouldn't serve them. My father drove me to Greenham one day and took me to the local Little Chef to get a meal. They wouldn't even serve him because he was with me. People were quite aggressive and we were always referred to as 'those dirty women'.

––––

Greenham women became used to harassment from the police and local council. But instead of breaking their spirit, the experience had a radicalising effect.

––––

STEPHANIE CHAMBERS

The police and the US Army were definitely abusive. They called us 'dirty dykes'. They enjoyed arresting women who were doing nothing more than protesting against the missiles, and dragging them away, off site: women would disappear for two or three days that way – held in a police station but never charged. It was just harassment.

SÎAN JAMES

I got evicted from Greenham. What would happen was that women would be in the tents and the local authority would come around and slap eviction notices on them. The notices ordered us to leave the site completely. The next morning, they brought rubbish lorries along and threw anything that wasn't on the public footpath into the back of the machine to get scrunched up: tents, bedding, clothing – anything. But they couldn't legally evict us from the public footpath so we all got very good at moving our stuff on to the footpath quite quickly and it was really exciting to take part in the activities there.

STEPHANIE CHAMBERS

It changed my attitudes, politically: it opened my eyes. Because those Greenham women – not so much me but the women there day in, day out – did so much to get the American bombs out of Britain. But you never hear about it: it's women's history and that doesn't get talked about.

———

The protests at Greenham Common encapsulated the mood and divisions within Britain in the early 1980s. To those on the left, it represented a defiant stand against a jingoistic and repressive government, while the nightly television pictures of feminists and lesbians challenging the power of the State re-enforced a belief on the right that the country was facing an internal threat.

Mrs Thatcher's policies reflected that belief. She began to implement key parts of the Ridley Plan. The first prong of her attack was a new law that targeted unions, which she believed were undermining Britain.

The 1982 Employment Act allowed employers to sack employees who went on strike. But, even more crucially, it repealed the eighty-year-old legal protection, which insulated unions from court action if their members withdrew their labour. The new act allowed courts to seize – or 'sequester' – union funds in instances of 'unlawful' strikes.

The second prong was tough policing. The government secretly revived the largely dormant National Reporting Centre at New Scotland Yard. This was re-tooled to create a well-drilled and co-ordinated police response to handle 'flying pickets' in the event of a major national strike.

There was little effective opposition in Parliament to these increasingly hard-line right-wing policies. The Conservatives had a majority of 144 in the House of Commons. The Labour Party, meanwhile, had been hit by the defection of right wing MPs to form the Social Democratic Party (SDP) and was deeply split between the traditional centre-left and Militant Tendency, a new, radical Trotskyite movement.

DAVE LEWIS

I didn't really want to join the Labour Party: I felt it was too mainstream for my political views. And so I began moving towards the revolutionary left and Militant: I found a home in it for many years. Then Militant wanted me to join Labour, so I did.

I was very unimpressed when I went to the first few Labour Party meetings: it was all very mundane and full of people who seemed ancient – though they were probably only in their fifties – talking about municipal swimming baths and libraries. And that wasn't what I thought of as political: I was into the anti-apartheid movement and campaigning against nuclear arms.

———

Militant and other revolutionary left-wing factions, like the Social Workers Party (SWP), were committed to campaigning on the streets as well as in Parliament.

———

MARTIN GOODSELL

I had always been left wing and always considered myself to be a communist. I joined the SWP when I was very young. This was a time when the National Front (NF) took to the streets in London. There were some big confrontations, like the Battle of Lewisham, where the fascists were stopped from marching by the local community. The SWP was involved and I remember thinking, 'I just want to be part of this.' It seemed to me that this was a better way to be – a better society, people working together, co-operating, and we wouldn't have all these wars and conflict.

I became active in the Anti-Nazi League, which was then an SWP-controlled organisation. In those days, the NF used to have a stronghold in Bethnal Green and there was a space we contested with them at the top of Brick Lane. They would be there every Sunday and the youth wing of the SWP would go up and try to occupy that space; take it from the NF.

We used to think we were a little bit hard. On Saturday nights we'd take some speed, stay up all night and then stay in the space where the fascists would come, to occupy it so they couldn't get it. There were quite a few altercations but the idea of actually hitting anyone – I couldn't bring myself to do that. I might think it's a good idea to stop them but I just couldn't imagine myself hurting somebody else. I find the thought of violence quite abhorrent.

———

In March 1983 the government moved Ian McGregor from British Steel to become chairman of the NCB. McGregor's reputation for savage cost-cutting and mass redundancies made it clear that the Mrs Thatcher was ready to take on the miners.

Arthur Scargill: 28 March 1983

'Mr McGregor is a hatchet man. The policies of this government are clear – to destroy the coal-mining industry and the NUM.'

The NUM President wanted a national strike to fight the anticipated pit closures. Foreshadowing what would happen a year later, he argued that the union's rule book allowed the national executive to authorise a series of area strikes, which, when joined together, would form a *de facto* national stoppage. But his opponents on the executive insisted on a full national ballot of union members: the result was disastrous – 61 per cent of miners voted 'no'.

The vote exposed a fundamental fault line that had developed between mining communities – a division exacerbated by an incentive scheme, built into miners' pay packets. Those working in the older, run-down coalfields – particularly in South Wales – received smaller incentive payments than those in more easily worked pits across the English midlands. It was a rift that the government would soon ruthlessly exploit.

As 1983 wore on, the government put in place its final plans for confrontation with the miners. Ferdinand Mount, head of Mrs Thatcher's policy unit, drafted a confidential memo in which he described unions as 'a politicised Mafia' and urged the Prime Minister to 'neglect no opportunity to erode trade-union membership.'

On Mrs Thatcher's instructions, the Central Electricity Generating Board increased its use of oil and nuclear fuel to generate power, while coal production was simultaneously dramatically increased – from 42 million tonnes in 1982 to almost 58 million tonnes in 1983. Huge stockpiles of coal were built up, largely at power stations, in readiness for a miners' strike.

———

JONATHAN BLAKE

One of the reasons that Heath lost the strikes in 1972 and 1974 was that there were no reserves of coal, so that he had to concede to the miners. By 1982 Thatcher had decided to goad the miners into another strike.

But she had got the Coal Board, under MacGregor, to offer masses of overtime: so the government stockpiled enough coal to get through two years of a strike. This time, Thatcher had made sure she would win.

CHAPTER SIX
GAY'S THE WORD

Mrs Thatcher's government was socially, as well as fiscally, right wing. It dismissed a Home Office recommendation that the age of consent for same-sex sexual activities should be reduced from twenty-one to eighteen and refused to decriminalise homosexuality in Northern Ireland, which had been excluded from the 1967 Sexual Offences Act. In March 1980 it also rejected an amendment to a Housing Bill that would have given gay and lesbian couples the security of tenure already accorded to heterosexual couples. But these decisions, which now seem archaic, reflected what were then the prevailing attitudes throughout the country.

————

RAY GOODSPEED

People talk now about the laws back then – the laws against

us. But it wasn't the laws that really did you in; it was social attitudes. It was the idea that gays were sad, ridiculous, child molesting and pathetic: all of those things together, somehow. Gay men were dangerous people, in grey Mackintoshes, who preyed on children. That was society's attitude.

———

In April 198, John Saunders, a maintenance worker at the Scottish National Camps Association, was sacked for being gay. He complained to the Employment and Appeal Tribunal but it upheld the dismissal, ruling that 'a reasonable employer might consider a homosexual person a risk.'

———

NICOLA FIELD

We were viewed with disgust and ridicule. That was around us all the time: we were shouted at in the street. I was once on the tube and a group of blokes hissed at me, 'Lesbian!' It was said in a threatening 'we know what you are and, when the time is right, we'll come to get you' kind of way. On another occasion – again on the tube – a group of Nazis started singing 'kill the queers, gas the Jews'. I wanted to stand up and confront them, and scream at them until everyone joined in. But my girlfriend – who was black – stopped me: I think she felt even more vulnerable.

STEPHANIE CHAMBERS

I knew that the world around me was really homophobic. This was the early 1980s, [when] to be out and proud meant you could get beaten up. That happened to me once: I was coming out of The Bell, a gay pub in London, with another woman and on the way home I was hit because I wouldn't let a man touch me. He was drunk – not that this should make a difference: he was trying to kiss and touch me and I didn't want that. So he hit me and I fell to the ground.

Even walking down the street hand in hand with a girlfriend was something I wouldn't do. I knew I would be beaten up if I did.

———

In spite of this prejudice and harassment, a vibrant gay scene was emerging in London. A new weekly newspaper, *Capital Gay,* began publishing, and Heaven, the country's first major commercial gay nightclub, which had opened its doors in 1979, was rapidly attracting huge – often hedonistic – crowds.

———

PAUL CANNING

There were bad things going on then. In some places the pretty police were still going. And people were still being fired, and there were gay murders. But it wasn't a catalogue of horror: there was a vibrant, exciting social scene in London. It wasn't like that ten years before but, in the early 1980s, it was all taking off. Heaven was enormous – a giant shop window of a place. It was really vibrant and you could live a whole life completely safely within that cosmopolitan scene in London.

BRETT HARAN

I'd come from a very closeted background so, when I moved to London with my first boyfriend, my eyes were suddenly opened to a whole new world of exciting possibilities. It was thrilling to see the many facets of gay life in London, from drag and leather bars and discos, to the younger alternative scene at The Bell in King's Cross – a place where I made many lasting friendships.

I remember going to The Coleherne pub in Earl's Court for the first time and seeing all the 'clones' – gay men wearing checked shirts, jeans and moustaches so that they all looked identical, hence the word 'clone'. I was completely fascinated. I'd never seen anything like this before – certainly not in Oldham. But my most overwhelming feeling was this sense of elation; of going to places where there were other young people like me and who were happy to be in their own skin.

MIKE JACKSON

One day I finally realised there actually wasn't anything wrong with being gay. And all the layers of self-oppression fell away. You could no longer tell me now that what I felt wasn't natural. It was like stopping banging my head against a brick wall and, of course, I then went from zero to a million miles an hour.

I was simultaneously incandescently angry and incandescently joyous. I could have sex and it could be guilt-free. I was only nineteen but it seemed like I had so much lost time to make up. I mean, I knew it was illegal for me to have sex – because the age of consent was still twenty-one – but, in a way, that also gave me a kick. And I went on this fantastic sex spree: it was wonderful.

———

In December 1981 the first death from a new and frightening disease was reported in London. A forty-nine-year-old gay man died in Brompton Hospital, after a three-month illness.

Time Out: 18 December 1981

A rare and dangerous disease whose victims are almost exclusively homosexual and bisexual men has hit Britain … His case is identical to a series of puzzling US reports collated by the federal Centers for Disease Control (CDC) in Atlanta …

Speaking at a scientific conference in Chicago last month, Dr James Curran, who leads a CDC task force dealing with the problem, said, 'Data suggests an epidemic of immuno-suppression is occurring, primarily among homosexual men' …

'We have to be careful not to be alarmist,' a London doctor closely involved said last week. 'The numbers we are talking about are very small. But I think this problem is going to become a large one.'

Though it would not be given the acronym for many months,[4] the death in Brompton Hospital was Britain's first official case of what would become known as HIV/AIDS. Many more soon followed.

---

[4] In the first year, the disease was variously knows as GRID (gay-related immune deficiency) and HTLV-III.

JONATHAN BLAKE

In October 1982 all my lymph nodes were up. I couldn't put my arms down by my side. So I went to my GP in the East End and she said, 'Shake my hand.' I shook her hand and she held it in a special way. She explained that this was known as the Sailor's Handshake. In times past, whenever a sailor on shore leave approached a prostitute, the first thing he would do is shake her hand in this special way: he was actually checking her lymph node at the elbow and, if it was up, that was a sure sign of syphilis and he wouldn't go with her.

I hadn't had a recent syphilis test so the doctor suggested I went for one. I went to Middlesex Hospital and they took a biopsy and it came back as HTLV-III (the precursor name for HIV) and that was the start of it: I was diagnosed. At that point, the doctors didn't really know much about the disease. All they knew was that this virus was attacking my immune system. But they didn't know why, or where it came from.

But in 1974 I had lived in America for ten months. Later, in 1981, I'd stayed in New York and San Francisco and got involved with the whole gay scene and the gay bath houses. And I realised that San Francisco was where I met my virus.

But what the doctors did know was that it was killing people. And so, basically, from that moment on, I thought I was going to be dead within about three months. They didn't actually 'give' me three months – but there was talk which indicated that.

My number was L1. I was 'Number One'; the first person at Middlesex Hospital to be diagnosed with HTLV-III. Every hospital had their own system and I don't think anyone has ever tried to piece together the whole numbering system to see who was first nationally but I was certainly an early diagnosee.

So I got my diagnosis in October 1982. In December I tried to commit suicide. I was going to do it the Roman way (largely because I didn't know any other way): I was going to lie in a warm bath, slit my wrists and slink off into oblivion. I got in the bath and everything was prepared. But I just couldn't do it. I am my mother's son: I seriously could not bear the thought that someone was going to have to come in and clean up the mess. So then I thought, 'Well, if you can't kill yourself, you better get on and live.' And that was really difficult because I had stopped going out: I felt unclean; a pariah. I had this killer virus and I didn't want to infect anyone. My self-esteem was on the floor and I really didn't know what to do.

_____

In May 1983 the *Sun* responded to the growing AIDS crisis with the headline: US GAY BLOOD PLAGUE KILLS THREE IN BRITAIN. Throughout the inherently homophobic tabloid press, AIDS was portrayed as punishment for 'immoral' behaviour.

Derek Jameson, (then) Editor of the Daily Star

'Fleet Street does not like homosexuals. They think it is abnormal, unnatural and evil because it is wrong.'[5]

---

[5] Quoted in: *The End of Innocence: Britain in the Time of AIDS';* Simon Garfield, Faber, 1994.

BRETT HARAN

In the right-wing and red-top tabloids, the attitude to gays was pretty vile – it was just appalling. AIDS was labelled 'the gay plague'. The implication was that AIDS was the product of 'the gay lifestyle' and gay men who contracted the HIV virus were not deserving of public sympathy or compassion.

In 1983, just after Cecil Parkinson, the government's Trade and Industry Secretary, had been exposed for having an affair with his (female) secretary, there was a cartoon in the *Evening Standard*: it depicted a Whitehall minion saying, 'You can cross Parkinson off the queer list, sir.'

I was involved in the Labour Campaign for Gay Rights and we were so outraged that this cartoon had appeared that we decided to do a zap protest at the offices of the *Standard*. We got some leaflets together with the aim of getting into the newsroom to challenge the journalists: we wanted to tell [them] that the cartoon was homophobic and to call on them to oppose homophobia in the *Standard*.

Amazingly, we managed to get past the guys on the main door of the building and got into the newsroom. Security was alerted and the next thing I knew I was being pushed up against the wall by some complete mollusc who had his hand round my throat, after which we were all unceremoniously ejected from the building. I don't think the *Standard* reported it but we made the headlines in *Capital Gay*.

PAUL CANNING

The *Daily Express* ran really horrible cartoons showing mincing gay men – I mean, really over the top; just horrible. So a lot of us invaded the *Daily Express* building on Fleet Street. We went right into the newsroom, shouted and turned some bins over. We didn't get nicked: you could do stuff like that in those days.

———

The growing vocal demands of 'minorities' – gays, lesbians and Afro-Caribbean citizens – in Britain's increasingly polarised communities were perceived as a threat to public order. At the Conservative Party conference in October 1982, a senior police officer warned delegates that society faced an existential problem.

Inspector Basil Griffiths, Deputy Chair of the Police Federation

There is, in our inner cities, a very large minority of people who are not fit for salvage … The only way in which the police can protect society is quite simply by harassing these people and frightening them so they are afraid to commit crimes.

That same month, Mrs Thatcher's government announced its intention to intensify prosecution of homosexual acts that fell outside the limited protection afforded by the 1967 Act. While that law made gay sex legal, most of the precursors to intercourse were still classified as 'procuring' and 'soliciting'. It was unlawful for two consenting adult men publicly to chat each other up; even exchanging phone numbers in a public place was deemed to be an arrestable offence.

RAY GOODSPEED

It was legal to be gay but it was illegal to ask. It was the same as prostitution: you could do it but you weren't allowed to ask anyone to do it – that was soliciting for an immoral purpose. You had to somehow come together spontaneously to be allowed to do it – provided there were only two of you and it was in private. And private meant in a locked room inside a house with no other person there.

––––

Within weeks of the government's announcement, the Metropolitan Police raided a private party in west London and arrested thirty-seven men. They were charged with engaging in homosexual acts that were 'not in private'. And the continuing discriminatory age of consent meant that lesbians and gay men faced legal risks that did not apply to heterosexual couples.

––––

RAY GOODSPEED

In 1983 I was twenty-four and I hitched up with a boy who was just about to celebrate his eighteenth birthday. He became my boyfriend for a couple of months and then he told his family.

And I was terrified: he was under what was then the age of consent – which was then twenty-one – and that could have meant prison for me if his family had gone to the police.

––––

If clubs and pubs like Heaven and The Bell were the heart of gay nightlife in London, a small bookshop in Bloomsbury was its intellectual centre. Gay's The Word had opened in 1979, specialising in academic texts on gay life and history.

MIKE JACKSON

Gay's The Word was central: it was really a community hub – and back in those days, there weren't many places like that. It was a meeting place, it had a coffee bar, it was very important. It was a place to which a young gay man coming to London just gravitated. I wanted to immerse myself in gay politics and I found it so refreshing to go there.

MARTIN GOODSELL

It had been started by an explicitly socialist gay organisation and it was always very open to the developing lesbian and gay communities. The Gay Young Socialists Group regularly met there: it was extremely welcoming to us and I think the staff even used to leave us to lock up in the evenings. It was also the place you went to get your papers and leaflets – the place where you could find out what was going on, as well as just call in for a chat.

MIKE JACKSON

It also had a notice board, which was really important: it had notices offering flat shares, which could often be really difficult for lesbians and gays to find otherwise because there was often hostility to out people trying to rent. So the bookshop was very important in providing that lifeline.

MARTIN GOODSELL

And it was *the* place where, as a gay man, you could find out about your own history: they had a fantastic stock of books imported from America – which was probably around five or ten years ahead of Britain – so there were ideas you could get hold of that wouldn't be available anywhere else. And then, of course, it was raided by Customs & Excise.

———

On 10 April 1984 Customs officers descended on Gay's The Word, with a warrant issued under an obscure nineteenth-century law.

———

COLIN CLEWS

The basis for this assault was the Customs Consolidation Act of 1876. Just as Mary Whitehouse had used archaic blasphemy laws to prosecute *Gay News* in 1977, the British government was using antiquated legislation to attack this gay-community bookshop. The 1876 Act is, in effect, a way of skirting round the provisions of the much more realistic Obscene Publications Act of 1959.

That allowed for a defence on the grounds of literary or artistic merit. The Customs Consolidation Act, on the other hand, did not allow such a defence to be applied to imported material.

———

Since the British gay publishing industry was still in its infancy, much of Gay's The Word's stock was necessarily imported. Customs officers took away at least one third of the contents of the bookshop and seized £12,000 of stock, which was then in transit.

The impounded material included works by mainstream

international authors Tennessee Williams, Gore Vidal, Christopher Isherwood and Jean Genet. The criminal charges brought against the shop's directors increased fears of persecution in the gay community.

——

RAY GOODSPEED

The first Gay Pride march I went on, there were only a few thousand people and, to get enough support, you'd hand out leaflets and round up all the queens you knew on the scene. But their reaction would be, 'Oh no: you Gay Pride people – you're just causing trouble. Much better to keep quiet and unseen, then we'll be OK.'

I was even thrown out – ejected – from a gay pub in the East End for handing out Gay Pride leaflets. They didn't want to cause trouble: I was told that, if we gays just kept quiet, the police and the government would leave us alone.

As soon as we started marching down the street, 'they' – the people in the straight world – were going to make trouble for us all.

——

The community did start a fighting fund for Gay's The Word. But, despite the increasing hostility of the right-wing government and press, there was little political support for gay men and lesbians on Britain's left.

——

RAY GOODSPEED

Politically, the Tories were anti-gay but so was Labour. There was no appetite in the Labour Party for gay rights at all at the time. Working-class trade unionists were no fonder of us than the Tories were. So I didn't particularly see the Tories as my enemy as a gay man: I didn't see is as 'Thatcher vs Gay people': I just knew that nobody liked us.

DAVE LEWIS

In 1983 I got a motion adopted by the Labour Party Young Socialists (which was dominated by Militant) in favour of lesbian and gay equality. But it wasn't adopted by the national party. I don't think it was anti-gay bigotry that stopped this; it was just that the party didn't think the issue needed to be given a huge amount of attention. The situation had been that way for about a decade: gay rights just hadn't made its way forward enough. It just wasn't something that the leadership felt was important enough to discuss. There were people inside the party who felt this was a personal, not a political, issue.

NICOLA FIELD

There were women's sections, which I was a part of, who were pro-LGBT, but the main party itself was resistant. I felt like I was in a rebellious group trying to bash down the doors of the system. I think the party saw us as outside the norm, living on the edge of society, and people didn't want to be associated with us.

We were trying to pull the Labour Party into having an understanding of equality and it was very resistant: I had the sense that it didn't want us. It seemed to think we would bring down the tone of things.

In February 1983 a by-election was held in the south-London constituency of Bermondsey. Labour's candidate was Peter Tatchell – then primarily known as a left-wing activist. The Party persuaded him not to speak openly about his homosexuality but, despite this, he was subjected to a vicious smear campaign. Male campaigners for the Liberal Party candidate wore badges bearing the slogan 'I've been kissed by Peter Tatchell'.

The Liberals won the election and, when Tatchell complained of a homophobic witch hunt against him, Neil Kinnock – who would shortly become Labour leader – was reported to have said, 'I'm not in favour of witch hunts but I do not mistake bloody witches for fairies' (Kinnock later denied making the remark).

———

MARTIN GOODSELL

At that level in the party leadership, even on the soft-left like Kinnock was, there was antipathy to gays. Back then, coming out as gay meant crossing class boundaries and there was this belief that working-class people wouldn't support all these 'metropolitan' types – meaning gays.

BRETT HARAN

I think the attitude of the Labour Party was that they didn't want to be associated with what the tabloids and the Tories were calling 'the Loony Left': they felt that identifying with this thing called gay rights was just going to re-enforce the message that the Conservatives were pushing – that Labour had lost touch with ordinary people.

Even more left-wing communist or Trotskyite organisations, like Militant, failed to understand the need for gay rights.

MARTIN GOODSELL

In fairness, the far left was just as bad as the Labour party – if not worse in some cases – in terms of anti-gay prejudice. The idea in the far left was that homosexuality is not a working-class thing. There was that mentality.

DAVE LEWIS

Militant had a problem with 'workerism'. Its mantra was that lesbian and gay equality wasn't an issue which was of interest to working-class people.

There weren't very many 'out' gay people, as I was, in Militant. I started pushing this in London and, with an informal network of members throughout the country, we began to push to get this on the agenda.

RAY GOODSPEED

Militant was not a particularly pro-gay organisation. It wasn't exactly anti-gay; it was just utterly dismissive of the question of homosexuality. That was seen as a personal issue with no relevance to working-class politics at all. I think I was the first person ever to stand on a Militant platform and talk about gay rights and talk about 'us' rather than 'them'. And I was greeted with total silence: total silence.

What I found was the people who were most bothered about me being openly gay were full-time Militant workers, full-time revolutionaries, primarily from middle-class backgrounds. They would say, 'Don't talk about gay stuff because the workers don't like it: the workers just don't like it.' There was an assumption that homosexuality was a purely middle-class issue and something of an affectation.

But, of course, when I spoke to a Militant summer school, which was full of working-class boys, recruited off dole queues – skinheads and kids from the streets – they were absolutely fine with it. And I realised that it was the people who professed to be speaking for the working class who had a problem: real workers were fine about homosexuality.

MARTIN GOODSELL

In the early 1980s I'd go up to Oldham to visit Brett's family. We'd go to bingo and a lot of the bingo callers were quite camp and there were also drag acts: in working-class communities drag acts were always quite a big thing.

Drag was acceptable as entertainment – and possibly a safety-valve for homosexuality (and attitudes to it) within a community. In some ways, it was a matter of: the more camp a person was, the easier it was to be accepted – people could fit them in a box, so to speak. The difficulty was more for gay men who weren't like that; those who might appear to have had a dark, hidden secret – that was probably more problematic because, for a lot of working-class people, being gay meant being effete and being upper class, if you like. And coming out did launch you into a much wider society: not that you forgot where you came from but it meant you could have a middle-class boyfriend.

In the absence of official Labour Party support, local authorities in Manchester, Southampton, Birmingham and – especially – the Greater London Council (GLC) took the lead in promoting equal rights for gays and lesbians. Under its leader, Ken Livingstone, the GLC affirmed gay rights as part of its anti-discrimination policy, and established the London Lesbian and Gay Centre. But this brought it into conflict with the Labour leadership – and with the tabloid press.

_____

PAUL CANNING

The GLC was really important. When I was running the Labour Campaign for Lesbian and Gay Rights, we worked out of Ken Livingstone's office – we had a corner in his office. And because the Tories and the tabloid newspapers made a big thing out of this, it was big news ever day. There was always something in the tabloids about 'children being indoctrinated' or 'lesbian colouring books' – things like that.

Some of it was overt homophobia but really this was a proxy war against Labour; they were attacking Labour with gays as the proxies. And that explains the hostility of most of the Parliamentary Labour Party to having anything to do with gay rights.

_____

Left-wing London councils provided both a safe place for gay men and lesbian women to come out and support for community-based projects.

NICOLA FIELD

I was active in gay groups. I was in lots of lesbian and gay groups: I was very active in the Lesbian and Gay Youth Video Project, which was supported by the GLC. We learned all about history and culture and socialist ideas and we produced *Framed Youth*. This was a film about young gay people's lives, which was shown on Channel 4 and at loads of festivals.

We went on marches and demos: CND, marches for abortion rights, in support of nurses and against cuts in the NHS. It was a tumultuous time: a time in which you started to pick sides.

———

Like the Labour movement, trade unions were also divided on tribal and industrial lines on the question of gay rights. Those in the relatively new administrative and public sectors were beginning to embrace the issue. But those serving traditional heavy industry were lagging far behind the times.

———

MIKE JACKSON

At that time, unions viewed gay men as shit, basically. The trade-union movement in the 1950s, 1960s and 1970s was huge but it was dominated by white, heterosexual men. And they were quite hostile to ideas like gay liberation and women's liberation.

WENDY CALDON

The unions were shockingly bad – especially the print unions and the miners. It was all 'guys, guys, guys' back then, very macho – in many ways, it still is. Gay people didn't really exist for them – except in old 'backs to the wall' jokes in the bar.

I knew that from my dad being involved in his print union (NATSOPA) – and the NUM was no different.

MIKE JACKSON

Within the union and left-wing political community, there was an awful homophobic attitude that homosexuality was alien to working-class people; that it was a middle-class thing and, in some way, middle-class homosexuals were corrupting working-class men. It also found expression in an attitude by some activists that homosexuality was a white man's thing because it didn't really exist in black communities. It was just blind prejudice every fucking which way.

BRETT HARAN

There was work going on inside some of the unions to support gay rights but many of us felt that we were swimming against the tide. A lot of union leaders felt that LGBT issues were peripheral. Gay rights wasn't seen as a serious issue; it wasn't a priority. My union, NALGO, was a bit different, probably because it was a white-collar union. But the more traditional, manual-labour unions were reflective of the attitudes in the community at large.

DAVE LEWIS

I don't think gay rights had ever been discussed within my union, the Transport Salaried Staff Association. It had never been on the agenda for discussion. And it was the same within the wider union movement: it was just an issue which had not been given any serious thought. The unions just didn't see it as significant enough to discuss and raise. Things were moving – but they were moving slowly. But the focus was only on non-discrimination: it didn't go any further than a policy that 'it would be wrong to discriminate against these poor things.'

———

It was against this fractured background that preparations for the most bitter and divisive strike seen in Britain for two generations began.

CHAPTER SEVEN

ENEMIES WITHIN

As 1983 drew to a close, both sides were preparing for a miners' strike. In the previous 12 months the NCB had closed 23 pits with the loss of 21,000 jobs.

In November 1983 the NUM introduced a national overtime ban. Seeing the writing on the wall, Arthur Scargill knew that the success of previous strikes in 1972, 1974 and 1981 had been founded on a shortage of coal for electricity generation. The overtime ban aimed to create a substantial cut in production and the reduction in the ever-growing stockpiles of coal at pitheads.

Then, on 1 March 1984, the NCB announced the closure of Cortonwood in South Yorkshire. The move came as a surprise. Cortonwood miners had been told their pit was safe for another five years; the pithead baths had just been refurbished and miners were still being transferred to the colliery from other exhausted pits. Nor was Cortonwood high on the official list of 'uneconomic' pits; a report by the Monopolies and Mergers Commission had placed it at ninety-second on the roster of mines most at risk of closure. The announcement was a gauntlet thrown down for the NUM to pick up.

Five days later, NCB chairman Ian McGregor increased the pressure. He told the NUM that, to reduce government subsidies, 20 more collieries would have to close with a loss of another 20,000 jobs.

His aim was plainly to force the union's hand into calling a strike: such savage cuts would inevitably mean that entire communities across the north of England, Scotland and Wales would lose their main source of employment.

A significant number of miners were already on a war footing: across Yorkshire the overtime ban had led to a rash of local disputes, causing the paralysis a major part of the coalfield. Scargill and his executive faced a difficult choice. If they didn't fight now, they never would but, equally, embarking on a national strike at the beginning of spring was bad strategy. Demand for coal usually dropped at this time and power stations had amassed substantial reserves.

On 8 March 1984 the NUM National Executive Committee met. By a vote of twenty-one to three, it backed the area strikes in Yorkshire and Scotland, and agreed to sanction action by any other area under the union's 'Rule 41'. This allowed the National Executive to build a succession of local strikes without calling a ballot. It would prove a fateful decision.

Nationally, the coalfields were divided: the majority of miners in Nottinghamshire, whose livelihoods were not threatened by the NBC plans, demanded a national ballot. Even South Wales – traditionally loyal to the NUM – looked doubtful.

———

HYWEL FRANCIS

At the beginning of March I was with the entire leadership of the South Wales NUM and there was absolutely no talk of a strike. Then, within a week, the whole British coalfield was in turmoil.

It was the most unlikely time for a strike: it was the end of the winter. Unlike in 1972 and 1974, [when] there had been a build up of overtime bans and planning for the strike, in 1984 there was none of that. And there was no proper ballot held.

DAI DONOVAN

The South Wales miners had tried to challenge pit closures before. There had been a number of sit-ins but we had failed to get the rest of the coalfields in England to support us.

JAYNE FRANCIS-HEADON

I was sixteen and doing my O Levels. There were rumblings about a strike and there were a lot of arguments in our house. My mum was frustrated and angry that it was all happening again. She had a go at my dad about coming out on strike and told him that he needed to sort things out. She didn't want the strike to happen but she knew it was going to so she became very frustrated. And she said to him, 'You're twenty years too late. You didn't come out when they closed the Seven Sisters pit in the 1960s – you're mad.' The fight for the Seven Sisters pit just hadn't been there and my mum couldn't see what this new strike would gain us and couldn't understand what was in the NUM's mind.

There was also this feeling that there was lots of coal here in Wales and that coal would always be needed. And there was also the fact that the Welsh pits weren't necessarily being threatened at the start of 1984, so my mum felt, 'Why should we go to fight for the English?' My dad was generally very quiet but, if he did say anything back, there would be an argument. So there was a lot of tension in the house.

————

In a ballot across the South Wales coalfield, eighteen of the twenty-eight pits voted not to strike. The local union leadership realised that pickets would be needed to stop some miners going in to work.

————

DAI DONOVAN

Although it's true that the strike was eventually 100 per cent solid in Wales, it wasn't like that at the start. It wasn't a case of everybody coming out on the Monday morning: some collieries had to be picketed out.

HYWEL FRANCIS

South Wales was initially opposed to the strike. So we had a battle to get our pits to come out. But once they did come out, the loyalty to the union was such that they were capable of being the coalfield which was the most solid. Our old history has something to do with that, but also the history of the closure programme from 1979 onwards: South Wales was right at the sharp end of that and was always trying to motivate the national union to oppose the pit closures.

DAI DONOVAN

I believed in the strike from the very start. The great tribute to the South Wales miners is that some of them didn't – they didn't share my politics even – but they believed in the union and, when the big whistle went, they came out.

CHRISTINE POWELL

We'd been watching closely in the week leading up to 12 March and my husband, Stuart, was realising he'd be coming out again. On the morning the strike started, I passed Blaenant Colliery on my way to work and I could see a handful of pickets and very few cars in the car park. Stuart was supposed to be on afternoons that week so I rang him from work and told him the pit was picketed out and he might as well stay in bed. His reaction was that all it meant was a few days off: in our experience, strikes only ever lasted a couple of weeks. So we didn't really worry at the start: and anyway, Stuart and I were totally in agreement that the strike was right. We were defending people's right to work; we were defending people's livelihoods.

———

On the day the strike began, miners and their families were given a foretaste of the forces ranged against them.

HYWEL FRANCIS

Once the South Wales coalfield decided – eventually – to strike, they mobilised immediately and miners went from here to picket in other coalfields. And, very quickly, the government realised the impact of South Wales pickets and so the police began illegally stopping people travelling.

COLIN CLEWS

I was living in Nottingham when the strike started and Nottingham was the epicentre of the working miners – the men who went on to form the Union of Democratic Mineworkers (UDM). They thought their pits weren't at risk of closure because they had some of the most modern collieries in the country. They were also very conservative anyway – and had been as far back as the General Strike. Because many of the pits in Nottinghamshire kept working, the county became a hotbed of activity, with flying pickets coming in. But, as a result, Nottinghamshire became a police state.

One night, when I was coming back from the pub, there were five of us travelling in a white van, which belonged to one of my housemates who was in a left-wing theatre group. We came to a major roundabout and, as we got near, we could see this huge convoy of police vehicles. It was quite extraordinary. And that became the norm: if you drove out of town, you'd have to go through a police roadblock. Sometimes they'd stop you, search the car and ask who was travelling with you – and even which party you'd voted for in the previous general election. There were stories of people's houses being raided in the middle of the night on suspicion of sheltering flying pickets.

CHRISTINE POWELL

When we picketed the steel works at Port Talbot, it was just after the murder of PC Yvonne Fletcher outside the Libyan Embassy in London.[6] As Hefina and I were walking down through the picket, I heard a policewoman say to her colleagues, 'They're just like the people who murdered Yvonne Fletcher.' And that was their attitude: we were like shit on their shoes. As bad as murderers.

And the attitude to the women – to striking miners' wives – was the worst: we were just rabble to the police. When we moved on to the roundabout just outside the steelworks, to shout at the lorries coming out through the picket lines, there was this young policeman and I saw that his knuckles were white with rage: he was struggling to control his temper. But you know how it made me feel? Proud. And I thought to myself, 'There's not many "rabble" who have a degree in physics, is there?'

———

The national press was almost universally hostile to the strike. Newspapers published spurious claims by the NCB that the pits across the country were defying the NUM. The *Daily Star* splash headline read, REVOLT GROWS IN PITS STRIKE, while the *Financial Times* declared, 'The attempt to usher in national

---

[6] PC Fletcher was fatally shot during a protest outside the Libyan embassy on 17 April 1984. Her killer fired the shots from inside the embassy.

industrial action has virtually collapsed.' Meanwhile, viewers of breakfast TV were told that Blair Hall Colliery in Scotland was working normally – despite the fact that it had closed down some years before.

————

SÎAN JAMES

I always used to say that there was a poison dwarf sitting in the corner of every one of our living rooms. It was television: a poison dwarf spewing out all these things. And suddenly, we were watching TV in a very different way. We were having to rely on the media for what was happening in other coalfields and we were realising that it didn't reflect anything that was happening; what our men and our husbands were coming home and telling us about being on the picket line.

CHRISTINE POWELL

I would go down to picket Blaenant at half past six in the morning, then I'd come home, have a shower and watch telly with my breakfast to see how many scabs had allegedly passed me that morning. The reports said there were loads of them, which didn't tally with the one or two I had seen while I was picketing, so obviously I had 'misinterpreted' what constituted a scab.

SÎAN JAMES

I realised this strike was going to be longer than the previous ones. We knew it wasn't going to be like 1972 or 1974, when it was six weeks and the government capitulated. We knew that this time we faced an intransigent government, which had deliberately picked the fight and the timing of it. Because none of us would have picked March; none of us would have picked a point when coal stocks were so high. One of the reasons why the strikes before had been so successful was the power cuts. This time they had prepared for that.

———

From the outset, Arthur Scargill's decision to avoid calling a national ballot divided the country and antagonised even those who were sympathetic to the miners' cause.

———

PAUL CANNING

Scargill should have held a ballot. If he had held a ballot, the whole basis of the strike would have been much stronger than it was. Politically, it was a complete bullshit move not to have one and, as far as I understand it, it was mainly about internal NUM politics. Which is just stupid. And Scargill has been a member of the Stalin Society – and I really, really hate Stalinists.

SÎAN JAMES

Now, I can see fault in Arthur and I've told him to his face what I think of him. And the way he lived wasn't like the way it was down here. It wasn't common for the union here to provide housing for its officials – and Arthur had the use of a flat in the Barbican in London, which the union paid for. That was a bit of an eye-opener. We didn't have that tradition at all in South Wales. We didn't know people – except politicians – who had flats in London.

But he knew there were big battles coming. Overtime had been cut to the bone and there was a work to rule in some pits. The big bonuses had finished; coal seams in places like Abernant had come to the end. So, even before the strike in 1984, we'd already been cut back to the bone. And I never heard my father or my husband ever criticising Arthur during the strike.

———

Political opposition to Mrs Thatcher's policies was also deeply divided. The Labour Party and its leader, Neil Kinnock – whose father had worked in the South Wales coalfield – were caught between historical support for the miners and Scargill's refusal to hold a national ballot. Meanwhile, the hard, or revolutionary, left was also split by internecine rivalries.

———

RAY GOODSPEED

When the miner's strike started, my immediate reaction was 'let's get out there, on to the streets.' I was in Militant and, like many other political activists, we immediately began collecting money for the miners – but in an absurdly sectarian way. The whole attitude was one of pretending that the rest of the left simply didn't exist. That meant we had to run around trying to find a street corner where there was no one else from any rival political group. We couldn't collect for the miners with anyone else – no: it had to be *our* collection and our collection only. It was the very definition of sectarian and it was stupid because where we were collecting, in Hackney, there were people queuing up to give money.

WENDY CALDON

I wanted to support the miners because I saw it as the same argument as rate capping. It was about defending communities, jobs and services, and fighting against Thatcher and her destruction of the welfare state. Same fight, no difference.

As soon as the strike started, there were workplace groups formed throughout councils all over the country to support the miners and raise money for them. I joined the one in Camden but it was very much dominated by male Oxbridge graduates who used to go around in miners' jackets with NCB on the back. They were committed but it kind of annoyed me because I was a working-class girl. I was really committed to the cause but I was sitting like a lemon in meetings while these men talked on.

———

While the left talked or bickered, the government and the NCB began to put their planning into action. The NCB took the first steps in legal action to sequester NUM funds over its refusal to call off flying pickets. And the re-energised National Reporting Centre began deploying thousands of police officers from London to the contested coalfields in Nottinghamshire.

———

HYWEL FRANCIS

In a struggle like this, without being melodramatic about it, you were really part of a resistance movement. There was a sense that this was to be 'The Last Struggle'. It was to be our 'Alamo'. People were very conscious of previous fights – particularly the 1926 strike. One miner said to me, 'We will win, won't we? Because history is on our side.'

But the problem with that is that it relies on a romantic view of the 1926 strike. I had been brought up believing that it was a great victory when, in fact – aside from the fact that the communities here had been able to sustain themselves for such a long time – it was a terrible defeat and it broke the miners' union for a generation. And, in that sense, 1926 paralleled what would happen in 1984–85. I don't think we realised the scale of the forces against us. It wasn't the government – it was the State. Every arm of the State was thrown at us, just as it had been in 1926.

SÎAN JAMES

Nothing prepared you for the Met. The way that the Metropolitan Police behaved: nothing prepared you for that. Nothing that I'd done, all the demonstrations and marches I'd been on: I'd been to some sticky places but nothing prepared you for the Met – nothing. In fact, I'd never really seen much of the police – not even at Greenham – before the strike. Mostly, I'd viewed them as just having a job to do – the evictions and what have you. And some were good and some were bad. But I thought they were just doing a job. And then came the strike and that changed our perception of the police.

I went on the picket lines in Nottingham and discovered that we weren't allowed to shout the word 'scab'. If we shouted that, we would be arrested. In the end, we worked it out so that one side of the road shouted 'sc–' and the other side shouted

'-ab'. And the police would run between us trying to catch someone actually saying the word. And I thought, 'This is bloody ridiculous. We're in 1984, in Britain.'

———

As spring turned to summer, clashes between miners and police intensified, culminating in June in a pitched battle at the Orgreave coking plant in south Yorkshire. Six thousand police, supported by dogs, corralled five thousand pickets into a field before sending in forty-two officers on horseback to charge and beat the miners.

———

DAI DONOVAN

The attitude of the police to us was awful – terrible. I've got a clean record as far as the police are concerned and I thought they were appalling. I've never forgiven them for what they did in the strike – and I never will forgive them. It doesn't matter what they say about only doing their job. History tells me that there was another nation where police said they were only doing their job – and it led to 6 million people being gassed. I've got nothing but contempt for the police. Don't get me wrong: I don't go out of my way to stick my fingers up at them but, during the strike, they were culpable. They were doing what Thatcher wanted and many of them enjoyed it.

———

The 'Battle of Orgreave' hardened resolve on both sides of the strike. But, away from the violence and drama of the picket lines, mining communities were facing a quieter and more insidious foe: poverty – and, with it, hunger.

SÎAN JAMES

When the strike started, the government had changed the benefit rules so that it was presumed families were receiving strike pay from the union. And, personally speaking, I couldn't figure out how we were going to survive.

CHRISTINE POWELL

There was no strike pay here in South Wales – never was. Where would the money have come from? The union couldn't just dole out money with nothing coming in from the other end.

SÎAN JAMES

By the end of the first month, there was just nothing coming in; there was just whatever little bit of money we had saved. And that went very quickly. And things like gas, electricity, telephone – let alone running a car – became very difficult to manage. Our telephone was cut off because we didn't have any money to pay for it.

DAI DONOVAN

The first few months were like a phony war and people struggled, but they managed and survived in the main through families and extended families. I don't know of anyone who actually starved in the strike – and certainly not at that stage. But after four weeks, the cycle of payments that people had to make meant people were in difficulties.

SÎAN JAMES

We started to look at things like food shopping in a very different way: we couldn't go and just put what was wanted into the basket. There were no packets of chocolate biscuits or strawberry ice creams – what we used to call 'nicies' in our family.

DAI DONOVAN

Into the third or fourth month, it was clear to me that things were starting to get tighter and I was worried that the strike could weaken. The quickest way it would crumble would be when people saw their families starving.

Our diets have never been great in Wales but very definitely seeing your family suffering would have had a bad effect on the strike. It wouldn't have had that effect on me: I had two kids but they would have bloody starved before I gave in. But for anybody who wasn't as committed as me, it could have.

———

With no union funding, and cut off from benefits or welfare payments, the beleaguered South Wales mining communities of the Neath, Dulais and Swansea Valleys were forced to rely on themselves.

———

JAYNE FRANCIS-HEADON

As soon as the strike was announced, the socialist part of my mum took over. Her attitude was, 'Right, we're out now – what are we going to do about it?' From then on, my mum was out of the house even more than usual, attending meetings [and] organising things in the community.

CHRISTINE POWELL

A couple of weeks in, one of the striking miner's wives started a little support group in Onllwyn. It had a collection to help a couple of the single boys who were out: they got no financial support from the union and weren't eligible for any benefits. So they had nothing. The support group then was doing nothing more than donating a couple of sausages and a few spuds so they could have sausage and chips for support.

But we soon realised that we had to become more organised. We found we were having to feed a thousand people, and you can't do that from people just giving the occasional can of corned beef or a box of Cornflakes.

———

But where would the money for food, electricity, gas and rent come from? It quickly became apparent that South Wales was not able – and perhaps not willing – to support its miners.

———

DAI DONOVAN

The critical difficulty in Wales was that you had 22,000 people living in quite a small geographical area and the economy had never been great. To get money from those people to support the strike – well, it just didn't add up.

Many people from Cardiff and Swansea told me they gave money every week but my impression was that we couldn't get money. My impression was that places like Cardiff couldn't wait to see the end of the coal mines, despite the fact that the very economy of Wales had been forged by those mines and the shipping of coal out of Cardiff and Swansea.

I know this is contentious but I felt that Cardiff was waiting for the new service and financial economy; that Wales didn't need manufacturing any more. There was never any doubt in my mind about the strike but I began thinking strategically about how it could be pursued.

———

It was that strategic thinking which led, in time, to the hedonistic London gay community – and to one of the unlikeliest alliances in any industrial dispute.

CHAPTER EIGHT
FRIENDS WITHIN

For the traditional mining communities of the Welsh valleys, London was impossibly remote, both geographically and culturally; many miners – let alone their families – had never visited the capital, knowing it only as a place to which some of their children had fled and never returned.

————

SÎAN JAMES

Many of our working-class friends had left their backgrounds here and gone to London because they could live different lives there. Some did have supportive families but, to live their lives as they wanted to, they had to go to London. But for most of us, London was just a place that was full of money: we thought that everybody must be very wealthy to live in London.

But as the strike dragged on towards the summer, miners from all over the country began arriving in London to raise funds for their communities.

———

DAI DONOVAN

I went up to a political march about the strike in London and I saw people collecting money in buckets at the side of the road, and there were £5 notes and £10 notes in them. It turned out they were miners, collecting money for the Kent coalfield. And I thought, 'We should do that.' Because I saw the sheer amount of money that went into those buckets, before my eyes, in just a couple of miles.

I came back home and suggested to Hywel that we ought to do the same; that we ought to go to London to look for money to feed our families.

HYWEL FRANCIS

We had done some local fund-raising but we had realised that we couldn't raise sufficient money locally. We knew we had to go beyond our own locality. But the problem was that we were not allowed to go to London; we were told by NUM headquarters that we were not to go there.

In his wisdom, Arthur Scargill divided the world up and we in South Wales were given Ireland as the place to raise funds. Yorkshire and Kent – the 'favourite' coalfields – were given the whole of North America and London.

DAI DONOVAN

The NUM had given the London area exclusively to Kent. So that meant three collieries in Kent had the whole of London to sustain them when every other colliery in the country had peanuts. I thought that was ridiculous. I thought, 'This place can sustain us all if we ask for help.' That's why London was so important: I knew it could sustain us for a year – and that this would be impossible without London.

HYWEL FRANCIS

So we held a meeting and decided that, without telling the South Wales union leadership, we would send Dai Donovan up to London under the radar, so to speak.

He was told not to contact big trade unions or constituency Labour Parties. Instead he was to connect with individuals who were supportive of the strike – whether they were teachers or local government workers or whatever.

But he was given the clear instruction that, if anyone – union officials, for example – challenged him about making connections in London, he was to say that he was there strictly on his own initiative. And so, by the summer, Dai was based in London all week, building networks within trade-union branches and hospitals and the like. This resulted in small donations steadily trickling in to us back in Onllwyn.

––––––

But support for the strike was fractured and divided. Even other unions were hesitant about committing themselves to support the miners' cause – in part because they feared their own funds could be at risk if they did so.

———

GETHIN ROBERTS

I was involved in my union and was putting forward motions to meetings for us to support the miners. But the big unions didn't do so. There was a complete lack of commitment – partly because of poor leadership, partly because the laws had changed and secondary picketing was illegal. But my view was that they should still have done it: yes, their assets could have been sequestrated but they should still have done it. We should have had a general strike. I felt angry and bitter and let down. All of us who supported the miners felt that, and we felt impotent because we couldn't do what was so obviously necessary, which was getting all the trades unions out.

COLIN CLEWS

At the time, the left, as a broad movement, was incredibly factionalised and riven by in-fighting. From my earliest involvement with politics, I'd been acutely aware of which group was splitting off from which other group, of who was at odds with his former best mate and denouncing him as 'a running dog of capitalism'.

———

But inside the vibrant gay community – under frequent attack from press and politicians for its sometimes hedonistic lifestyle – an unexpected determination was building.

DAVE LEWIS

The scene in the early 1980s was quite tribal. There were 'cloney-type' venues, and drag in the more mainstream venues. And if you didn't like wearing leather or singing Diana Dors songs, you were a bit stuck really. It was liberating but a bit samey. I was twenty-one, twenty-two, and I didn't really feel I had arrived at my natural home. The whole hedonistic side of the scene passed me by: to be honest, I didn't like it – I was a bit of a puritan – and I shunned it. I didn't feel comfortable with the single-mindedness of the hedonistic scene. There were people whose lives revolved entirely around the gay social network but I didn't want to be that person. I wanted to be political and so slowly I began picking up a group of gay friends who shared my left-wing politics.

COLIN CLEWS

It was that whole experience of what Thatcher was doing to us that led us to support the miners. It was solidarity. We had to stand together. There was a lot of talk at the time of 'the Loony Left' – mainly within the Tory Party and its friends in the national press. I saw the opposite: I saw 'the Raving Right', who were coming up with completely ludicrous scare stories. I remember one was that the whole aim of gay rights was to put homosexuals into children's nurseries and indoctrinating the children into being gay, which, according to this nasty myth, contributed to the spread of AIDS. There were Tory councillors and Tory MPs who attacked the idea of giving homosexuals equal rights because this was a recipe for spreading AIDS.

BRETT HARAN

I very definitely saw a parallel between the way we, as lesbians and gay men, were portrayed in the newspapers – as deviant, a threat to 'normal' society – and what the miners were now experiencing at the hands of the Tory-supporting press. They were coming under attack in a way that we'd been used to.

The Tories were mobilising their friends in the press to undermine the strike and make it seem like this was a completely undemocratic thing and that Scargill had bullied the miners into going out on strike. I took the view that this was all part of the Tory propaganda war. The miners were on strike and it was all hands to the pumps as far as I was concerned. I instinctively felt that I wanted to make common cause with them.

COLIN CLEWS

During those first three months of the strike, I was finishing my social-work course, but I was always trying to think of ways to raise money for the miners. I'd taught myself shiatsu massage so I set up 'Massage for the Miners'. I put up a postcard in my local radical bookshop. It was £5 and all the cash would be sent to the striking miners. Well, in the end, I made £25. But I wasn't put off: I still wanted to do something to help.

STEPHANIE CHAMBERS

My politics were not rigid or dogmatic: it was much more about a sense of natural justice. I never joined any political party or movement. I didn't know the SWP from the Trotskyites. I was completely naïve – I didn't have a clue.

But I knew it was just so *unfair* what Thatcher was doing to the miners. That must sound lame but that's how I felt – it was just so unfair. And I also knew that, if she could do this to the miners, she could do it to anyone.

JONATHAN BLAKE

I wanted to support the miners for all kinds of reasons but some of it was because I completely understood what they were facing. I mean, here was this group of people who were basically the aristocracy of the working class. Their pay had always been good: now here they were being treated in ways that we had constantly been treated – perhaps even more so. The weight of the State was down on them.

CLIVE BRADLEY

The very first demonstration I'd been on was the Grunwick Strike and mass picket in 1977. At one point, a chant went up – 'the workers, united, will never be defeated' – and the reason was that the NUM had turned up. There was this contingent of NUM coming down the street.

RAY GOODSPEED

For the union movement and the left in general, the NUM was our Green Berets; our Paratroopers. In the early 1980s there had been strike after strike in industry after industry, which had all been defeated. And everyone was holding their breath waiting for the miners. We believed that the miners would be the 7th Cavalry coming over the hill to save us all from Thatcher.

But to turn this nascent, instinctive support into something tangible meant overcoming unease about the absence of a national ballot.

———

GETHIN ROBERTS

My personal view of the NUM was that there was a failure of leadership and that national ballot would have made a difference, and would have resulted in an overwhelming vote for strike action. I can understand the argument against it but it did hand a gift to Thatcher, presentationally.

———

There were also deep suspicions about the NUM leadership and some of the union's traditional attitudes.

———

GETHIN ROBERTS

I think it's true to say that the NUM was hostile to gay issues. Homosexuality was seen as 'un-manly', and the NUM tradition (and that of all blue-collar unions) was all about machismo. There was also a large element of homosexuality being seen as a 'bourgeois deviation' – a public-school thing forced on the working class. But people generally in those days were brought up to be unthinkingly homophobic: lesbians and gay men were seen as perverts.

NICOLA FIELD

The union newspaper the *Miner* used to have a page-three nude in it. A woman I know went on a picket line in Yorkshire and was told to get her tits out for the lads. And she told them that they weren't going to win this strike with those ideas.

COLIN CLEWS

I volunteered at my local strike centre. I knew one of the women who worked with the Women's Support Group. [The organisation] had been contacted by the strike centre, saying it needed a typist. My friend rang me and suggested I applied so I turned up the next day at the Nottingham strike centre and said I was volunteering to be the typist. The looks of disbelief were priceless: the reaction of the striking miners and the union officers was 'What did you say? There must be some mistake.'

It wasn't that they were hostile, or even suspicious; it was just the concept of a male typist which just did not compute. Still, they let me in and I worked there for a few weeks.

They didn't know I was gay – they were intimidated enough by the fact that I was a bloke and a typist without telling them I was homosexual as well. The whole atmosphere in the strike centre was one of extraordinary machismo and gender-based assumptions.

_____

Three months after the strike began, the annual Gay Pride march was due to parade through the streets of London.

_____

JONATHAN BLAKE

Gay Pride marches were always in June, and I always went. At the time, HIV was my whole world: I believed I was dying, actually. For gay men then, it was like what it must have been like in World War One. People were dying and dying horribly: it was terrifying.

I thought to myself, 'You're going to be dead in a week so you can do anything. Anyway, 'Pride' was part of my calendar, so I went. And that Gay Pride march is where the whole LGSM thing started.

––––

A few days before the march, Mark Ashton – a young, flamboyant gay-rights activist and communist – decided to use 'Pride' to raise money for the striking miners.

––––

MIKE JACKSON

Mark was working as a kitchen porter in a hospital at the time. Although he was passionate about his politics, he could suddenly switch to humour and he was also so mischievous. At one point he had worked at the Kings Cross Conservative Club in full drag for six months. But he was also working as a volunteer at Gay Switchboard. He interviewed me when I applied to become a volunteer and I realised that we shared a socialist perspective as well as being gay campaigners. We quickly became good friends.

One day I bumped in to him at Kings Cross station. He just came out and asked if I fancied getting hold of some buckets and collecting money for the miners at the Pride march the following Saturday. I thought it was a good idea, said yes, and that was it.

RAY GOODSPEED

I was on the march when Mark Ashton and Mike Jackson turned up with buckets to collect money for the miners. Most people like me had already been collecting money for the miners – in our workplaces or in our unions – and 'Pride' was just another place to collect: it was meant to be just a one-off thing. But it went so well that we thought, 'This is interesting. Maybe this can go further. Maybe we can make a bit of a movement out of it.'

MIKE JACKSON

We were astonished by the responses we got from people on the march. The strike by now was three months old and the miners' families were really beginning to suffer. We were astonished by the generosity of people giving money but even more so by what they said to us. It turned out there were an awful lot of people there who hated Thatcher as much as we did. They told us explicitly that they hated her.

In those days, Pride used to end at the University of London Student Union, known as ULU. That afternoon a meeting had been arranged where a young Kent miner was due to speak. The room was packed – it was standing room only. And I thought, 'Wow! Who knew there was this much support for the miners within the gay community?' So on the strength of all this, Mark put a little classified ad in *Capital Gay* calling a meeting at his house the following Sunday, 15 July. And that was where it all started.

BRETT HARAN

One day after the 1984 Pride march, my partner, Martin, saw an advert in *Capital Gay* asking people to come to a meeting to see how we could drum up some support for the miners. I'd already been involved in collecting money for the miners through my union (NALGO) and I was also involved in the Gay Young Socialists. But I had this urge to do something more to support the miners.

It was an instinctive thing: it felt like a declaration of war – this was the Tories absolutely nailing their flag to the mast and I thought we had to take a stand. I had a real sense of this being an 'us and them' situation: the battle lines had been drawn and so, when the LGSM advert appeared asking people in the gay community to do something, it seemed perfect.

RAY GOODSPEED

There were eleven people at that first meeting. I was then – and still am – what you might call a 'class-struggle queen'. What drew me to LGSM was precisely the link with working-class struggle. I was involved in other gay groups but it was the class-struggle element of LGSM which really attracted me: that's what I had been looking for all my life. I didn't see this as a struggle that gay people specifically needed the miners to win. I saw it as a struggle that everybody – especially the working class – needed the miners to ride in and save us from Thatcherism.

–––––

A month later, LGSM held a full inaugural meeting. It established a written constitution based on a simple overriding principle.

Lesbians and Gays Support the Miners Group: Constitution, 2 September 1984

The aim of the group is to organise amongst Lesbians and Gay men in support of the National Union of Mineworkers in its campaign against pit closures and in defence of the mining communities [and] to provide financial assistance for miners and their families during the national miners' strike.

Meetings are held weekly and are open to all Lesbians and Gay men and delegates from affiliated organisations … Decisions are normally taken by consensus, but if a vote is needed a simple majority suffices.

To establish itself on a legal footing from day one, LGSM knew it needed to set up a dedicated bank account.

Minutes of the Inaugural Meeting of Lesbians and Gays Support the Miners

Open bank account with Co-Op Bank. Constitution to follow lines of Labour Campaign for Gay Rights – this is necessary to open an account. Income [to be] from sympathetic organisations and collections.

———

DAVE LEWIS

The Co-Op then was quite progressive. They were the only real option for anyone on the left. Can you imagine what the reaction would have been had we headed for a mainstream high-street bank saying 'Hello. The Shirtlifters and Cornholers against the Bomb would like to open an account, please'?

MARTIN GOODSELL

It would be more of a problem these days, I suspect. If I went to a bank and asked to open an account for lesbians and gays to support a political group like the miners, we'd have to jump through quite a few hurdles. In fact, banks are closing down the accounts of some international solidarity groups.

———

The next challenge for LGSM was what to do with the money raised on the Pride march: none of the young activists had any direct connection with the striking miners. Nor did it seem wise to send the money directly to the NUM: the union had just been found in contempt of a court banning it from disciplining officials who broke the strike. No fine had been imposed but it was clearly only a matter of time before NUM funds would be sequestered. A new mechanism had to be found to channel cash directly to the striking communities.

———

DAI DONOVAN

I'd identified that we needed to set up a system that maintained the fund-raising even when we weren't physically in London. So that meant we needed to set up a system of support groups there who collected money regularly and sent it to us in South Wales. We called it 'twinning'.

MIKE JACKSON

We were initially at a loss about how to get the money to the miners. We knew we couldn't send it to the NUM because its assets were at risk from sequestration. So we knew there was no point trying to work with the union itself. We had to twin with a mining community, rather than supporting the union. But how? I remember shrugging my shoulders, not knowing what to do.

RAY GOODSPEED

We'd got all this money but we didn't really know what to do with it. But one of the people who attended the LGSM meeting was a Communist Party member and he knew Hywel Francis, who had also been in the Communist Party and was part of the South Wales support group in Dulais. And so we had this link and thought, 'Why not Dulais?'

HYWEL FRANCIS

I was in the front room of my house when I got a phone call from the secretary of the Communist Party in Wales. He told me had a message from a group of gays in London, one of whom was from South Wales and had left the valleys because there was more 'space' to be gay in London.

This group of gays had been raising money but couldn't make a link with a mining community that was prepared to recognise and respect them. There were plenty of people who would have taken the money but they wouldn't perhaps have been prepared to acknowledge the relationship with a group of gays. I was fine with this and said yes. So I sent Dai Donovan up to meet the gays.

DAI DONOVAN

One day Hywel said to me, 'When you're next in London, there's a cheque to be picked up from this group of gay people.' At that point, gay rights hadn't crossed my path – not personally.

But I was aware of some people's attitude to gay people. I was always keen on history so I was familiar with the story of Alan Turing – perhaps before many other people became aware of what had happened to him.

And I'd been aware of anti-gay sentiments in the newspapers, and the overriding impression these gave was that gays weren't nice people. But I didn't think anything much about it. I just said I'd pick up the cheque, because there was no difference in my mind between them and any other group that supported us. So I arranged to meet Mark Ashton and Mike Jackson for a coffee at a Wimpy Bar just across the road from Paddington station. We spent about an hour and a half or so chatting, and only spoke about the strike and about politics. And what was remarkable was the degree of synergy between my thoughts and the LGSM people I met.

_____

After handing over the cheque at that first meeting, LGSM wanted to put the relationship with Dulais on a formal footing. But the young gay activists were far from sure how their request would be received.

_____

RAY GOODSPEED

Our guiding principle was unconditional support for the miners and their families. We didn't do it to get something back. Of course, we hoped for a response of some kind but we kind of thought they'd say, 'Oh, thanks very much – now fuck off, you pansies.' But it didn't matter: we were going to support them even if they had said fuck off.

MIKE JACKSON

At that point, the people in Dulais didn't know of our existence. So I wrote to Hefina Headon, who was secretary of the Neath, Dulais and Swansea Valley Miners Support Group, asking if we could twin with them.

HYWEL FRANCIS

I'd sent Dai to meet the gays and planned to explain it all to the support group later. But by the time I went and put the case to the meeting, a letter had arrived, addressed to Hefina, from Mike Jackson.

SÎAN JAMES

The letter came in among all the other letters we received. Our arrangement was that all the letters that arrived during the week were read out at the Sunday meeting so that everybody knew what was happening.

When the letter was read out – when the meeting was told it was Lesbians and Gays Support the Miners – there was a lot of tittering. It was like a nervous laughter that went around the room. And I remember thinking to myself, 'Why are people laughing?' And I could see a lot of other people thinking, 'Why are we laughing?' Because there wasn't any particular reason – apart from the name.

HYWEL FRANCIS

Sîan says that people laughed when the letter was read out. I don't remember that but the minutes[7] of the meeting show that clearly there was some kind of frisson about the idea. And from there on, things moved very quickly.

SÎAN JAMES

Now Hywel will tell this story in a different way. And the minutes of the meeting were sanitised: I'll always remember that the minutes were sanitised. I wouldn't say it was nasty – there was nothing like 'we don't want that type here' or 'we don't want their money'. But at this point, there were jokes like, 'Well, boys, we'll all have to stand with our backs up against the wall.' It was the men who said all this, not the women. It was just very, very macho and this is where the macho nature of the community came out.

My own attitude was that I didn't care who these people were: they had gone to the bother of raising this money for us so we can jolly well accept the money and say, 'Thank you very much.'

---

[7] The minutes of the support group written bluntly and robustly by Hefina Headon are part of the Coalfield Collections in Swansea University's archives. They reveal a remarkable picture of solidarity, as well as the underlying tensions within the group.

CHRISTINE POWELL

Then Dai stood up and said he'd already made contact with them. Silence. Shock. I mean gays were people who existed elsewhere.

Then there was a little ripple – a titter of laughter – and Dai got all defensive because I think he knew in advance what the reaction was going to be.

DAI DONOVAN

I can honestly say to you that I was never – never – curious about their sexuality. What was important to me was that they were helping us. And I had the additional thought that we should be grateful for their support because of the attacks they'd been exposed to: attacks which many miners were only just being exposed to.

––––

Those attacks were about to increase dramatically. Towards the end of July 1984, Margaret Thatcher gave an incendiary speech to Conservative Party MPs.

The Times: 20 July 1984

The Prime Minister last night drew a parallel between the Falklands War and the dispute in the mining industry. Speaking at a private meeting of the 1922 Committee of Conservative backbench MPs at Westminster, Mrs Thatcher said that at the time of the conflict they had had to fight the enemy without; but the enemy within, much more difficult to fight, was just as dangerous to liberty …

On the miners, Mrs Thatcher was unbending. She said that the message she was receiving from all quarters was that militancy must not win.

———

CHRISTINE POWELL

I remember hearing Thatcher call us 'the enemy within'. And I thought, 'If she is calling us that, I'm *proud* to be the enemy within.'

HYWEL FRANCIS

We were not the enemy. Not at all. In fact, the way we worked together and supported one another, we believed that our values were the best values that we in Wales embrace, and the best that all of British society embraces.

CHRISTINE POWELL

These men [the miners] got up in the morning, went down a hole in the ground to dig out black stuff so people could watch their tellies and turn their lights on. These men paid their income tax, they supported their kids, they supported their local shops. And these men were now called the enemy within. Forty years before, they had been the saviours of the country, producing the coal for the war effort. Hero to zero. To me, it's still a no-brainer. All these men wanted to do was work – an honest day's work for an honest day's pay. What's so awful about that?

BRETT HARAN

Thatcher's statement didn't remotely surprise me. It just crystallised in my mind that this was a titanic struggle and that she saw it as a battle to the death. She clearly wanted to demonise the miners. She wanted to create this narrative in which they were seen to be inimical to the life of the country, and that they must be defeated because they represented some greater evil – a threat to democracy itself.

COLIN CLEWS

It was part of that whole Thatcher-generated hatred: this fear that society was under attack and there was a threat from the enemy within.

The Soviets and the Argentineans threatened our Empire and our security from without, and the rabble – people like us and the miners – threatened the country's moral fibre from within.

DAVE LEWIS

I suppose I expected nothing less of her. I hated Thatcher with a vengeance and anything she didn't like was something I could learn to love. I wasn't surprised at the intolerant language that she and the rest of the cabinet were using about the miners. I didn't perceive the miners as the enemy of the State: I did think the State was definitely the enemy of the miners.

HYWEL FRANCIS

In those difficult times, it was calculated that not much more than 30 per cent of the British population supported the miners. So, in an odd sort of way, we often felt that the other 70 per cent were 'the enemy within'.

SÎAN JAMES

The important thing we had learned was that, if we were being vilified, if we were being denigrated and if the State was calling us 'the enemy within', what did that say about all these other people who, we'd been told for years, were also the enemy within? Perhaps they were just like us. Perhaps they were being unfairly treated. Perhaps they were being lied about. And our perception changed dramatically.

DAVE LEWIS

I do see the irony, though. Back then, I was a revolutionary socialist. I did perceive myself as the enemy within – and I was proud to be so. I would have done anything to undermine the Tory government.

COLIN CLEWS

We hated the Tories and we hated Thatcher and we saw her bullying someone else other than us. It's the same thing as seeing a little old lady being mugged on the street: you'd just go and help her. And that's how it was with Thatcher and the miners and LGSM.

BRETT HARAN

I just knew that, whatever it took, she was going to deploy

those resources to defeat the miners. So, just as the Tories had done, I decided to nail my flag to the mast. I thought, 'If this is about opposing what she represents, and her government represents, I'm in.'

CHAPTER NINE

SOLIDARITY

From the outset, LGSM focused on tapping into the generosity of London's gay community.

––––

DAVE LEWIS

I had already been heavily involved in collecting for the miners – every Saturday for four hours – through the Labour Party. But what I hadn't really considered before was bringing the miners' case to the lesbian and gay community.

So my reason for joining LGSM came down to raising money for the miners, but also raising political support within the lesbian and gay community. And by standing outside gay venues and shaking a bucket, LGSM was bringing the case to their doorstep.

The young activists began with an announcement in *Capital Gay*, appealing for support.

'Support The Miners': *Capital Gay*, 20 July 1984

The miners' strike is now in its twentieth week ... they and their families depend entirely on donations of food and money from people who support them and wish to show solidarity with them. We are a newly formed group of lesbians and gay men who want to take part in that show of solidarity.

We want to demonstrate to the lesbian and gay community the vital importance of supporting the strike and the reasons why a victory for the miners will be our victory too ...

Many will say that the miners are notoriously anti-gay but, if they see us actively supporting them, showing solidarity with them, their attitudes will change ... There may soon come a day when people like the miners will come to our aid ... we hope that you will help us.

———

MIKE JACKSON

I remember the first time we unfurled our LGSM banner – a huge, heavy thing that Mark had made for us. It was at the national women's demo in support of the miners. We were on the Embankment in London and there were thousands of people around us.

CLIVE BRADLEY

We argued that we needed the miners to win. If the miners lost, the Tory government would be going for everybody, and our lesbian and gay communities would be an easy target.

MIKE JACKSON

We were very nervous as we unfurled this vast banner – Lesbians and Gays Support the Miners. I was thinking, 'Oh God, how are all these people going to react?' Remember people hadn't seen anything like it before.

And people started pointing at us and the banner. And then they started clapping. And that was wonderful. I felt that 'OK, this will work. People get it.'

———

But not everyone did get it. Within days, the pages of *Capital Gay* carried a hostile response.

'Would The Miners Support Us?': *Capital Gay*, 3 August 1984

I must protest about the 'silly eleven'. Support the miners indeed. They (Lesbians and Gays Support the Miners) should ask themselves how much support they would receive from the miners if the situation was reversed. Have any of them lived in a mining town or community? I would say not or they would know of the false machismo of both men and women ...

As for spending money (whose money?) on print-outs for support to the miners ... it could be spent on better, more needed causes such as our gay defences, our gay old and lonely, our AIDS victims.

'The miners will never identify with us': *Capital Gay*, 17 August 1984

'If ever there was an example of inadequate people trying to gain strength and support by latching on to another, totally irrelevant cause, this must surely be it ... There is no police/government versus the gays running battle as they would have us believe ...'

'Stick to what you are good at': *Capital Gay*, 17 August 1984

'You will soon have to change the name of your newspaper from *Capital Gay* to 'The Red Flag' if you continue with articles such as 'Support The Miners' ... Wake up, gay papers, and stick to what you are good at – reporting gay events.'

———

JONATHAN BLAKE

There were an awful lot of gay people who were Tories and supported Thatcher. Not all gay people are supporters of the left.

———

LGSM activists would soon encounter this same hostility as they shook and rattled collection buckets on London's streets.

Meet LGSM: Mark Ashton working on the LGSM stall at 1985 Pride festival in London (*above left*), Brett Haran and Martin Goodsell (*above right*), and Nicola Field and Stephanie Chambers, both wearing their Pits and Perverts benefit gig t-shirts (*below © Nicola Field*).

Above: The picture that gave birth to the dancing scene in *Pride*. Sîan James (in the long floral dress) applauds Jonathan Blake's footwork, in the Onllwyn Miners' Welfare Hall, October 1984. Jonathan made the pink chequered trousers he is wearing in the picture himself. © *Imogen Young / People's History Museum*

Below: 'DYKES + FAGGOTS SAY RIGHT ON ARTHUR!' From left: Gethin Roberts, Mark Ashton, Robert Montgomery and Mike Jackson.

Above: LGSM members picket the Neasden Power Station in London, winter 1984. From left: Jonathan Blake, Mike Jackson, Ray Aller, Colin Clews & Ray Goodspeed.

Below: LGSM members Johnny Palmer and Rob Cooper collect for the miners at Camden Town tube station. Police intervened, confiscated all the money collected and arrested Johnny, holding him for over an hour and then releasing him without charge.

Above: LGSM unfurl their banner at 1985 Gay Pride march (directly under the banner, from left, are Jonathan Blake, Nigel Young and Stephanie Chambers). Behind them, the miners' banner from Blaenant Lodge NUM is visible.

Below: The historic moment in which the miners joined thousands of gay people to march at the 1985 London Lesbian and Gay Pride parade.

Above: A force of nature: Hefina Headon (played by Imelda Staunton in the film *Pride*) pictured with her daughter Jayne Francis-Headon (left photograph) and her hero, miners' leader Arthur Scargill (right photograph). © *Jayne Francis-Headon*

Below: Cliff Grist speaks at a South Wales miners' welfare hall. Cliff, played by Bill Nighy in *Pride*, was a pillar of the mining community in South Wales but his sexuality, whilst known and accepted, was rarely mentioned. LGSM's arrival would change everything for him.

Above left: Food to feed the valleys was stacked inside Onllwyn Miners' Welfare before being divided into thousands of weekly food parcels. © *Christine Powell*

Above right/below: Until LGSM donated a minivan, the miners' support group used any available vehicle to distribute food parcels throughout the valleys. This Mini Metro was stacked with 269 pints of milk and 269 loaves of bread.

© *Christine Powell*

FREE

CAPITAL GAY

28 pages!

Friday December 14th 1984   A WEEKLY NEWSPAPER PUBLISHED BY GAY MEN   Number 172

British AIDS total goes over 100 cases

he total number of AIDS cases in Britain has gone ver the psychological milestone of 100 cases.
The Department of Health told us this week that the total number now 102, of whom 44 people are dead.
The number of cases is following the American pattern almost entically with a doubling of the figures every six months. That eans we have to plan for 400 cases within a year.
The Department of Health said the increasing numbers of cases "worrying" but that it was "too early to tell what the long term

effect might be. We hope it will be less than in America".
The Terrence Higgins Trust described the figures as "depressing", and John Eldridge, a member of the Trust said: "We urge gay men to read our new leaflets and to consider ways of reducing the risk of getting AIDS.

Protection

-The most important points are to cut down the number of partners and to avoid anal sex, except perhaps with regular lovers.

"We don't yet know how much protection condoms give against HTLV-3 transmission. They may offer some protection but we worry about the possibility of them tearing or coming off. Thus, if at all possible, it's best to avoid fucking altogether."
They hope that gay pubs, clubs and shops will stock their leaflets, which are also available by sending an SAE to BM AIDS. London WC1N 3XX.

See also Meldrum on AIDS on page 11 and other articles on pages 3, and 17.

1,400 pack major benefit concert at the Electric Ballroom

BRONSKI BASH NETS £5,000 FOR MINERS

Jimi Sommerville in the audience before going on stage; and, inset, miner David Donovan

The 'Pits and Perverts' concert at Camden's Electric Ballroom on Monday raised nearly £5,000 for mining communities in South Wales and Yorkshire.

Ticket touts appeared as queues formed down Camden High Street; the event, organised by Lesbians and Gays Support The Miners, was completely sold out, and £4.50 tickets were fetching £15 and more.

About 1,400 people were there and the door takings, destined for the village of Dulais, near Swansea, raised £2,500.

Inside, the foyer looked more like a street market, with stalls from organisations such as Housman's Bookshop and GAYN Records.

Headlining the event was Bronski Beat, with lead singer Jimi Somerville grinning and positively sweating with pleasure at the party atmosphere the group was whipping up. As Eisenstein's classic silent movie, *Strike*, played appropriately in the background, he ran through the packed crowd's favourites from *No More War* to *Ain't Necessarily So*. Devotees chanted 'Pink Singers . . . Pink Singers . . .' demanding the backing group to this last item.

The four-hour event featured nearly all the major performers from the alternative cabaret circuit. Ransome, Andie Oppenheimer, Bernard Padden and the Nervous Kitchens, opera from the Vauxhall Kunsttheater. The most rapturously received were

By Eric Presland

Strange Language and The Moonlighters.

Strange Language are two very funny women. Alice and Viv, dressed in nightshirts and using lots of daft props, performed, among other things, a weird punk-ish electronic version of *Tea for Two*. The highlights of The Moonlighters' set were about sexist building labourers (*The Men Who Swing From The Scaffolding*), a kind of calypso, and a paean to shoplifting (*I Just Can't Help Myself*), dedicated to Sainsbury's in Stamford Hill.

The raffle, which raised £900 for Dulais, offered as prizes mementoes from the music business, including framed Gold Discs from The Specials and Bronski, plus a dress of Mari Wilson's and a signed photo of Lenin (who unfortunately wasn't able to be there in person).

But the most emotional moment of the evening came when compères Kate Thomas and Nigel Young introduced members of the mining communities for whom the evening was raising money. To cheers from the women in the audience, Hefina Headon of Dulais declared in ringing tones:

'The women of South Wales have been liberated. We had no idea of the power we had. That will not be suppressed. We will never go back to sitting at home again.

Never forget

Collections raised over £1,000 for Kiveton Park in South Yorkshire, and David Donovan pledged that the miners would never forget where their support had come from. "You have

worn our badge, 'Coal not Dole', and you know what harassment means, as we do. Now we will pin your badge on us, we will support you. It won't change overnight, but now 140,000 miners know that there are other causes and other problems. We know about blacks, and gays, and nuclear disarmament. And we will never be the same.

As the crowds drifted away, a tireless Jimi Somerville was still rattling the collecting buckets on the door, and visiting miners were pinning on 'Pride '85' badges to wear into the night.

CAPITAL GAY

WATCH out for next week's special festive *Capital Gay* with Christmas fun and games and all the listings for Christmas and the New Year.

In common with other papers *Capital Gay* will not publish during the holiday period. After next week's paper (December 21st) there will be a gap before we publish again on January 11th. Our office will be open for business from 10am on Thursday January 3rd.

Details for inclusion in our special Holiday What's On column must arrive – in writing – by 5pm on Monday December 17th.

INSIDE

CAPITAL GAY
38 MOUNT PLEASANT
LONDON WC1X 0AP
PHONE 01 278 3764
(3 LINES)
TELEX 261177

CAPITAL GAY READERS AWARDS on page 13

'Mark was a very popular guy - he knew everyone', says close friend

We speak to friends of late gay rights icon Mark Ashton to find out more about the Portrush man ahead of 'Pride' release

Feature

NICHOLA NEILL
nichola.neill@coleraintimes.co.uk
@coleraine_time

As we exclusively revealed last week, a new movie 'Pride', set to be released later this week, will tell the story of how a Portrush gay rights campaigner helped the Welsh miners back in the 1980s.

Mark Ashton was brought up in the resort and attended the Catering College before moving to London.

While there Mark became a gay rights activist, and during the 84/85 miners strike, Ashton and his friend Mike Jackson, set up 'Lesbian and Gays Support the Miners' (LGSM).

In doing so they raised over £20,000 for the mining families of the Dulais Valley in South Wales and helped to break down prejudices.

Sadly Mark died of HIV in 1987.

This week, The Coleraine Times spoke to one of Mark's oldest friends Robert 'Monty' Montgomery, who studied with him at the former Portrush Catering College.

He described Mark as 'loud and in-your-face' but added that he had loads of energy.

Monty joked: "Mark was always the 'Belle of The Ball' and that's because he knew everyone."

Looking back on growing up in Portrush with Mark, Monty recalled: "Punk was happening and he embraced it like there was no tomorrow.

"He was by far the best dancer at the local clubs (Kellys, now Lush! Portrush and Chesters) where our group had a reserved booth next to the DJ.

"The bouncer Tommy, a Scottish Hells Angel, made sure that we weren't hassled by anyone.

"Mark would watch the off duty soldiers busting out the Northern Soul moves and within a few minutes he could follow them step for step...with a bit of an Ashton twist!

"Being gay in Northern Ireland at that time wasn't something you made public, however I recognised a kindred spirit in Mark and the two of us began the process of coming out, first to each other, then our friends."

Monty went on: "It was hard not to be political living in Northern Ireland at that time as the civil war raged across the province.

"Portrush was a unique place in that although it was predominately a Protestant town, the kids at the Catering College and the nearby University of Ulster in Coleraine, coming from all backgrounds, could mix together in peace - often it was the first time that

> **"Mark was always the Belle of the Ball and he knew everyone."**

Film in focus: Mark Ashton.

some had met people of a different religion.

"This environment had a profound effect on Mark.

"When we completed college, Mark and I jumped on the first boat out of Northern Ireland, set sail for Liverpool and ended up in London.

"Mark hung out with people like Boy George, Marilyn, Phillip Salon, he frequently cross-dressed, living as a woman for about six months when we shared a flat on Ladbroke Grove.

"He never left the house unless he was in full drag, and he was totally convincing.

"Morning ritual was getting out of bed, consulting his book of Hollywood glamour portraits and choosing a look for the day.

"He had his eyebrows shaved off and would with the quick flick of a eyebrow pencil have 'the look'."

Monty went on to talk about Mark's political background: "I was aware of his political involvement, first through his work at the Young Communist League, in which he went on to become the first out gay man to be on the General Secretary, and then LGSM.

"I myself became involved in LGSM shortly after its inception."

Above: The *Coleraine Times* features a story on the remarkable Mark Ashton, who hailed from nearby Portrush, on the Northern Irish coast.

Below: Gay's The Word bookshop, in Bloomsbury, was where LGSM met until they outgrew the space, holding all-day Saturday bucket collections outside throughout the strike. Always more than a bookshop, Gay's The Word fought off raids by the police and was a community hub for LGBT people across London and the South-East.

RAY GOODSPEED

The bare minimum was doing one collection – either a couple of hours outside Gay's The Word or a community centre. But mostly it was outside gay pubs. Collections had to be outside – even in the cold weather – because the pubs didn't want their customers hassled.

MIKE JACKSON

We used to get abuse sometimes in or outside gay pubs. You got the full gamut of people who supported the miners and people who didn't.

COLIN CLEWS

My memory of the bucket collections is that people in the streets were generally supportive. There were a couple of gay men who would do that whole 'what have the miners ever done for us?' thing. No lesbian ever said that to me but a couple of gay men did. Other people walked past and sneered but no one ever stopped to have a full-on argument.

DAVE LEWIS

We did get into discussions – and sometimes arguments – with people. There were people who were antagonistic: they were of the view that 'why should we do this for the miners when they've done nothing for us?' And there was also the view that 'we should be raising money for our own, because there's people dying now.' This was the whole AIDS things. People were very good about telling you what you ought to do but not so good at actually doing it themselves. But it was exciting to have those arguments.

JONATHAN BLAKE

We collected outside Gay's The Word, and the shop is on a thoroughfare: it wasn't just well-wishers who went by. And there were times when people would curse us out. But there were others who were supportive and gave money and engaged in conversation with us.

MIKE JACKSON

Gay's The Word was quite good, but I remember collecting outside there one day in November. It was just shortly after the tragic incident when two young lads – striking miners – had chucked a concrete slab off a motorway bridge in Wales and a taxi driver taking a strike-breaking miner to work was killed. So I'm outside collecting with a few others and an old man came past, pointed at us and shouted, 'Murderers!'

COLIN CLEWS

The only incident I had involved the police. They turned up and told us that we couldn't collect on the street in front of Gay's The Word. The manager of the shop had told us that, if we stood in a particular position – on the glass skylights directly in front of the shop – we only needed Gay's The Word's permission to collect there. And that was the case legally. But the police came round and told us we had to stop or they would arrest us and think of a charge on the way back to the police station.

It was a power play by the police. And so we'd stop, step inside the shop and wait till the police had gone away before starting to collect again.

And, of course, the police would come back again an hour or so later and we'd go through the whole nonsense again. I think the police didn't like both the fact that we were gay and that we were collecting for the miners. They saw us as a bunch of poofters supporting these subversives – the epitome of the enemies of law and disorder.

From previous dealings with the police, I certainly had no doubt that they were homophobic. They might have called us 'sir' when asking us to move on but it was said through gritted teeth and with a certain menace.

RAY GOODSPEED

The other people who argued were gays who'd come from mining areas. Not all of them: we found that people who came from this background were split pretty much fifty-fifty between those who would willingly give £20 and those who said, 'I came from a pit village or town – I hate those homophobic bastards. They made my life a misery – I ran away from London to get away from them and they can die, they can rot in hell. Come on, Margaret Thatcher.'

STEPHANIE CHAMBERS

It could be hard work, collecting for the miners. It wasn't like we were collecting for a dying child; it wasn't for a hospice for children. It was for striking miners – and it could be hard work.

Sometimes we got abuse from people. I don't know if it was the old 'what have the miners ever done for us?' It was more 'F off.' But at least there was never any physical abuse.

JONATHAN BLAKE

You never collected on your own. It was always in groups, and that was for safety because we were queer, we were collecting for Lesbians and Gays Support the Miners, and there was always the possibility of being queer-bashed.

And, of course, we had all the money we'd collected – so that could have been a double-whammy for anyone who wanted to attack us.

——

As summer turned to autumn, LGSM's activists found that responses to their collections varied depending on the nature of the gay venue they targeted.

——

GETHIN ROBERTS

Generally speaking, outside gay pubs and the bookshop I got an extremely positive reaction but, at nightclubs like Heaven, it was much more mixed. Some people would be completely dismissive or worse, antagonistic.

RAY GOODSPEED

Heaven was the main commercial gay nightclub. It didn't like us very much and didn't like us collecting there. It was run by big businessmen and many gay businessmen opposed the miners because they [the businessmen] were Tories.

GETHIN ROBERTS

A lot of people at Heaven weren't involved in politics at all – gay or otherwise. They were what we termed 'Scene Queens' – people whose lives revolved around consumerism, fashion and hedonism, and that part of the scene. They were older and more affluent than the people who went to pubs like The Bell, who were often unemployed and had very little money. Yet they contributed a lot and were very much more generous than many of the richer gays who went to Heaven.

And, as an institution, Heaven was not supportive: we got hassled by the door staff and told to move on.

BRETT HARAN

I think, initially, there was a certain amount of amusement that we were collecting for the miners outside Heaven. It's not the sort of thing anyone would have expected as they queued up to go into a gay nightclub. Sometimes we got comments like 'what are you doing collecting money for the miners? What have the miners ever done for us?'

PAUL CANNING

But there was one night when the lesbian who was the 'door bitch' at Heaven made everyone – whether they were a Tory MP or whoever – put some money into the bucket. Every single one. It was a question of 'You want to come in? You want to meet "Mr Right"? You put some money in the bucket. If you don't pay, you don't come in.'

RAY GOODSPEED

It was a similar thing outside the leather bars in Earls Court. They were full of middle-class queens with their bikes and their leathers and they would give us a bit of mouth about the miners and how Thatcher was going to win.

They were openly pro-Thatcher – nothing to do with them being gay; it was purely a class thing. There was a gay group inside the Tory party and they would have been part of that if they were part of anything.

MARK ASHTON

It's quite illogical to say, 'Well, I'm gay and I'm into defending the gay community but I don't care about anything else.' It's important that, if you're defending communities, you also defend all communities. The miners dig coal, which creates fuel, which actually creates electricity. One of the reasons I support the miners is that they go down and do it. I wouldn't do it. I mean, would you go down a mine and work?[8]

BRETT HARAN

I took it all as an opportunity to engage with people who opposed us; to point out that the miners were under attack just as we'd always been under attack and so we needed to make common cause. Sometimes I won these arguments, some times I didn't. I got pretty good at knowing the sorts of people it wasn't worth having a prolonged discussion with.

---

[8] Interview in *Dancing in Dulais*: 1985 LGSM video.

The divide between those who supported LGSM's effort and those who resented them extended to the gay community's stars and celebrities.

————

STEPHANIE CHAMBERS

On the whole, people were supportive and just put money into the buckets. But one day, a famous alternative comedian – who was known to be very left wing – came up, took £10 *out* of the bucket and ran off. Very odd.

DAVE LEWIS

I used to collect at a pub called The Union Tavern, at the Oval. I would do one collection on a weekend and one midweek. I'd get something like £4 – in 1980s money – in a collection. Lily Savage used to perform there twice a week: she was very supportive of the miners' cause on stage and would often talk about it in character to the audience.

Paul O'Grady [Lily Savage's alter ego] had seen me shaking the bucket outside a couple of times: he always gave money and offered a few words of comfort, but could see that the collections weren't raising a huge amount of money. And so on two or three occasions, he wouldn't let anyone leave the bar until they put money in the bucket. And the collection went from four quid to twenty-five quid on those nights because everyone was absolutely terrified of Lily. I certainly was: there weren't that many things that frightened me then but Lily Savage was one of them.

BRETT HARAN

I was collecting outside The Bell in King's Cross one night when I recognised the film director Derek Jarman coming out of the pub. He didn't say anything but I do remember that he smiled as he dropped a folded note into the bucket I was rattling. I thought it was a tenner – which was an unusually large donation in itself – but as soon as I unfolded it, I saw that it was a £50 note. I'm not sure I'd ever seen one before. I was utterly astonished and wanted to thank him but he was off. I was really struck by his quiet generosity.

———

Gradually, LGSM became established within both the centres of London's gay nightlife and the communities surrounding them.

———

RAY GOODSPEED

We had a very high profile in the gay press and some coverage in the far left, revolutionary press: there seemed to be headlines about LGSM all the time. There was nothing at all in the straight, mainstream media. But the entire left was under-reported in the commercial press, so why would they be interested in a sub-section of the far left like us?

PAUL CANNING

We used to do collections in Brixton and the black community there was completely supportive and very generous with donations. I don't ever remember a negative reaction to the collections.

CLIVE BRADLEY

People would put a lot of money in the bucket to show solidarity – presumably money they didn't have in many cases. LGSM was the first really concrete example of how an autonomous movement of what we used to call 'the especially oppressed' could struggle alongside the organised working class and transform working-class consciousness in the process.

PAUL CANNING

The point about the miner's strike was that it was like the General Strike of 1926: the country was completely split – one side was 100 per cent behind them and the other side was 100 per cent against them. There was this real division in the country. And we felt that particularly in London because we had just had two big riots.

BRETT HARAN

As the months went by and we gained more publicity in the community, a lot more people seemed to make the connection. They could see that mining communities were under attack by the government and the police and that this was something that they had experienced.

––––

But as LGSM's membership grew, so, too, did political divisions within its ranks.

––––

DAVE LEWIS

LGSM was made up of all sorts. It was 'Heinz 57 Varieties' politically. The majority of people – though not all – had some level of political philosophy. Some were Trots, some were communists, some were Euro-communists, some were Marxist-Leninist communists. And of the Trot variety, there [were] all sorts. There was Militant, Socialist Organizer, Socialist Workers Party, Workers' Power – loads.

MIKE JACKSON

Everybody has a different take on this but my memory is that, early on in LGSM, when we were attracting a lot more people to the weekly meetings, tensions – discussion and sometimes heated argument – grew between the rival factions of the left: Communist Party, Labour Party, SWP. I hadn't been a party-political animal since I left the Labour Party in my late teens so I was at a bit of a loss sometimes trying to determine and interpret the nuances between them all. I relied a lot on Mark, although I knew that he wasn't impartial, since he was a leading Young Communist League member. But I shared with him my fear that the group might tear itself apart.

MARTIN GOODSELL

My take is slightly different to Mike's. I think the initial group of people were all on the same page. We all realised that the miners' strike – and the need to feed people, sending money and food parcels – was the primary concern. There was nothing else as important as supporting the miners.

In the early days, there was no real antagonism. But as we became more successful, newer people joined and that's when people came in from other organisations. And they didn't do as much of the donkey work as the originals – the collecting, for example. I think they saw it as a political opportunity, rather than supporting the miners.

RAY GOODSPEED

Mark Ashton's politics were sort of Euro-communist: he was really into this whole thing of 'linking autonomous communities'. I never really got that. It seemed to imply to me that you had the working class over on one side and gay people somewhere else. That didn't really work for me because the way I saw it was that loads of working-class people – and loads of miners – were gay. So, although I adored Mark, there was always a bit of tension between us.

––––

To put a stop to the arguments and potential splits within LGSM, Mark Ashton wrote a clear statement of purpose, aimed at re-focusing the group on its overriding goal.

––––

MIKE JACKSON

When he brought it to the meeting, he'd rolled it up into a scroll and, before he read it out loud, he unfurled it, which raised a few giggles. That was so Mark: simultaneously deadly serious but with a bit of camp melodrama.

––––

LGSM Resolutions: 2 September 1984

Lesbians and Gays Support the Miners is a single-issue, solidarity group and owes no allegiance to any political party. The only requirements of members are that they are either lesbian or gay – and that they support the NUM in their struggle against pit closures, job losses and privatisation. LGSM is responsible for its own running and costs, actions and politics. No person can speak on behalf of the group unless it has been previously agreed by a 60 per cent majority at a full meeting …

———

MIKE JACKSON

It was a wonderful resolution. It said that LGSM is open to all lesbians and gay men regardless of party political affiliations or none, who support the miners and the NUM. The only requirements were that you supported the miners, that you collected for them, and were either lesbian or gay. End of story.

MARTIN GOODSELL

Mark's concern was that LGSM would get caught up in political discussion that wasn't relevant to our main focus. It wasn't that the discussion was bad in itself; it just wasn't the right place for it. Our focus was on the collecting for the miners and their families and Mark's resolution said that, if you hadn't been out collecting that week, you didn't have a right to vote at the weekly meeting.

———

LGSM Resolutions: 2 September 1984

Money collected by members shall be sent to mining areas in order to combat hardship.

This means for food and clothes and anything else which the mining communities themselves decide to use it for. LGSM is not in a position to decide how this money shall be used – that is up to the mining communities themselves to decide.

———

NIGEL YOUNG

What impressed me about Mike Jackson and Mark Ashton was that they were always very clear about what they wanted to do. There was no messing about. They weren't going to be bogged down in dialectic: they were very, very focused on collecting money and that appealed to me because I could see that, if IS or SWP or any of the others got into it, the whole thing would become a nightmare of internecine warfare. Mike and Mark were very focused on doing something practical – collecting money.

JONATHAN BLAKE

For me, it was the doing which was important. I needed to keep active and not to keep thinking about HIV and the fact that I'd got this fucking virus. I just wanted to keep busy, keep dodging and hope the bullet flew past.

MIKE JACKSON

I think by this stage it was almost as if everybody wanted to stop fighting anyway because we realised we had something good here – something big – and it would be just pitiful to tear ourselves apart. I think that people realised the prize was worth it.

And after this, LGSM was transformed. We became so fucking efficient after that. We realised we had a fighting force – an incredible, coherent, comradely fighting force. And the gay community's respect for LGSM grew and grew.

———

With respect came donations. LGSM's collectors carted their increasingly heavy buckets, filled with coins, back to be counted and banked.

———

MIKE JACKSON
Martin Goodsell and Brett Haran handled all the money we'd collected and took it to the bank. Their arms are a couple of inches longer than anyone else's because the huge number of coins they had to transport [was] so heavy. They would plead with us to change the coins into notes before they had to bank it.

MARTIN GOODSELL
My abiding memory is the smell of the copper coins. Even today I absolutely hate that smell. The taste of it on your fingers. All of it: horrible.

———

But in the beleaguered communities throughout the coalfields of South Wales, those copper coins were desperately needed.

SOLIDARITY

As the months dragged on, Margaret Thatcher's government ratcheted up the pressure on the striking miners: financial hardship and hunger were its chosen weapons. LGSM's donations would soon play a vital role in keeping the valleys alive.

CHAPTER TEN
SUPPORT

Within weeks of the start of the strike, the villages of the Neath, Dulais and Upper Swansea Valleys re-organized the efforts of the support group they had set up to protect their communities from the coming hardship.

———

HYWEL FRANCIS

Our support group was set up towards the end of April. It was established after Hefina Headon and some other women from this valley went up to a big rally in Barnsley, which was being addressed by Arthur Scargill. There they witnessed the early mobilisation of coalfield support groups and so they came back home fired up with enthusiasm.

I must have spoken with Hefina about it and that led me to decide to set up a support group here. I went through my telephone book and rang everyone I knew, asking them to put a fiver or a tenner in the post.

CHRISTINE POWELL

In the beginning, people were just giving bits out of their own fridge or their larder but then it became financial donations. Initially, these came from locals – mainly ex-miners – but then they began to come in from all over. It was humbling.

I was teaching in a school in a very well to-do area in West Swansea. Being the wife of a striking miner there was like having landed from Mars. Some of the staff there did give money to our support group but they did it surreptitiously.

JAYNE FRANCIS-HEADON

Once the group started, the women in the villages descended on it: they all just wanted to be part of the support. After a while – a few weeks – it was decided to have a women's support group. They would be about things to do with the children of the community – parties for them, and trips away, for example – and setting up a 'nearly new' shop – which was a jumble sale that was a permanent shop.

HYWEL FRANCIS

Right at the beginning, I realised that the men should not take the lead in the support group. The women were right behind the initiative anyway and I saw that, if we were to be successful, a lot of the power needed to be in their hands. And remember: many of the women here had far more experience of fighting for their rights than the men. The miners had largely inherited their rights from previous generations of trade-union struggle. But the women had had to fight for them much more recently.

Also, from the outset of the strike, it was plain that we were entering a period of great uncertainty. No one knew how long it would last and the communities were fearful of what would happen – and of debts rising up. And I saw that, unless the women were empowered, the strike was doomed. So that's what we did.

CHRISTINE POWELL

We had a meeting every Sunday afternoon in the miners' welfare in Onllwyn. And everybody wanted to come to that meeting. Hefina was secretary and in charge of taking minutes; I was treasurer, sitting in the corner and noting down in pencil whatever was handed in to me. My job was to take the money in and dole the money out.

———

As spring turned to summer, the support group saw families across the South Wales coalfield go from tightening their belts to suffering severe hardship.

———

JAYNE FRANCIS-HEADON

The biggest impact on us was that there was no money coming in. There was no money for anything. And that's when our food started changing.

DAI DONOVAN

That's when the necessity of food parcels began. It was clear to me that things were starting to get tighter and I was worried that the strike could weaken. The quickest way it would crumble would be when people saw their families starving.

SÎAN JAMES

We looked at other communities and they were running food kitchens. We never wanted to run food kitchens because we felt that they were very indicative of the 1920s – and a lot of people in our valleys remembered the soup kitchens of those days. We felt there was more dignity in providing food, and people could then use that to look after themselves.

HYWEL FRANCIS

The key thing was food. Food parcels hadn't been needed at the outset. But, of course, no one knew then how long the strike was going to last. So we started providing food parcels at the end of April. Early on there was a bit of… I wouldn't say resistance, but there were people who said, 'Oh, surely this isn't needed.' But, yes, it was needed: some families were near destitution.

CHRISTINE POWELL

Were people starving? There is no universal answer to that: my family wasn't, because I had a job, but others weren't in that situation. Everyone's circumstances were different.

HYWEL FRANCIS

Our principle in these valleys was that everyone should have the right to have a food parcel. It was a political principle: 'if you're on strike, you should have a food parcel. Irrespective of whether your wife is a teacher or a factory worker or a nurse, you all have it.' Now, the neighbouring support group two valleys away had a means test. Well, it was a recipe for disaster and it led to people going back to work because they felt they weren't being treated fairly.

SÎAN JAMES

One of the things we were most proud of was that every penny that was collected was divided absolutely evenly between the communities in the Dulais and Upper Swansea Valleys. And we also made sure that every family got exactly the same share. There was no means testing.

HYWEL FRANCIS

In some places, like Swansea, our information network didn't quite work as well as in the valleys themselves. And there was a handful of people there who became desperate. They didn't have the support of our communities: they were supposed to be looked after down there but they got lost in the anonymity of the city.

When one of our union officials reached out to these lads and went down to see them in their homes, he found that they were so hard up that they were burning their own furniture, and there was even a pair of child's shoes burning in the grate.

Unlike much of the rest of the South Wales coalfield, the support group set up in the Neath, Dulais and Upper Swansea Valleys was largely autonomous from the union lodges, which had traditionally controlled mining communities.

SÎAN JAMES

We would go off to other places and meet women who told us that the lodge decided how everything was going to be in the food parcels and the lodge would decide the value of the food parcels. They were being contained by the union and by the men. We were having such a different experience. And that was because, when we created our support group, we built into it the right for everybody to participate and everybody to have a vote. If you turned up to a meeting, you had a vote. There was no 'some votes are more equal than others' – everybody got a vote. So it didn't give the union or the lodge any advantage: if you turned up, whatever the subject under discussion at the meeting, you got to express your opinion and you got to cast your vote. And we just got on with it. Nobody complained that this is difficult; this is hard. It was what we had to do and we just got on with it.

HYWEL FRANCIS

The first thing was to take the issue of food out of men's hands. The local food co-ordinator in each village had to be a woman. It wasn't a gender thing; it wasn't an extension of the old thinking that a woman's role was in the kitchen. It was just common sense. If we were to have the full support of the women, they had to be empowered.

SÎAN JAMES

There were some pretty lively discussions. There was an argument about whether sugar was a luxury. We were discussing what to put into the food parcels: all the men said sugar was an essential but all the women said it wasn't – we knew we could live without sugar.

HYWEL FRANCIS

The men were clueless about shopping and the cost of food. Very quickly, we decided to set up ten food centres in each village in the valleys. Each support group was given an initial allocation of £1,000 from union funds to get it set up. Well, one of the local miners just went down the local shop and spent the thousand pounds on bags of sugar and loads of tea and tinned this or tinned that – and the women were furious. So there was a big debate about how stupid he was – which was true. The question was asked, 'So you've already spent this thousand pounds: where's the next thousand going to come from?' And the man said, 'Oh, the union will provide it.'

But the union was running a strike and wasn't going to be able to provide limitless money. Anyone with a shred of common sense would have realised that. There hadn't been strike pay even in the 1972 and 1974 strikes, and there was no strike pay in 1984. It was clear we had to do that ourselves. If the strike was to be sustained, we had to have an infrastructure, and the backbone of that organisation would have to be women – not least because, increasingly then, men from these valleys were away picketing other coalfields across Britain.

CHRISTINE POWELL

Every Wednesday, all the food came in to Onllwyn miners' welfare hall. The parcels for a thousand families were made up there and sent out to the other nine local distribution centres throughout the valleys in whatever cars we had access to. Each parcel would have pretty much the same thing: milk, a loaf of bread, Cornflakes, tins of corned beef – the basic staple foods you could make a meal out of.

HYWEL FRANCIS

We'd have our meetings every Sunday and each food centre representative would be asked how many food parcels they needed for the week. By the height of the strike, there were over a thousand food parcels. So we were feeding the equivalent of 4,000 people every week.

———

Then, in July 1984, the support group got wind that its bank account was about to be targeted in a forthcoming court action, brought against the South Wales NUM.

———

HYWEL FRANCIS

We were tipped off that something was about to happen. The union's funds were going to be seized and funds associated with the union might also be seized. And that's when we decided to put non-NUM people in as officers of the support group.

I had started as treasurer but we changed our chairman – who was an NUM official – and I was elected in his place. That took place on a Sunday and, lo and behold, the very next day our funds were seized – were frozen.

___

On 30 July 1984 the South Wales NUM was fined £50,000 for contempt of court after it ignored an injunction banning secondary picketing at Port Talbot steelworks. All South Wales Area NUM bank accounts were frozen, including those holding its hardship funds, as well as those of autonomous support groups across the coalfield.

___

CHRISTINE POWELL

We had our account with Lloyds Bank in Ystradgynlais, in the next valley. That night I got a phone call from Hywel. He said, 'They've sequestrated our money.' My reaction was incredulity.

HYWEL FRANCIS

We assumed Price Waterhouse – the huge accountancy firm appointed as sequestrators – had had access to information about our support-group bank account. In our view, that was against the law but it seemed the government had allowed them to do it. As a result, they knew we were raising a lot of money.

CHRISTINE POWELL

But Hywel also said we had an appointment with the bank

manager the next morning, so I spent hours that night going over the figures and making sure that the books were right.

HYWEL FRANCIS

I spoke to a law lecturer at Cardiff University and he volunteered to come to the valley to be our legal representative at a meeting with the bank manager.

CHRISTINE POWELL

We went over the next morning – Hywel, Hefina and myself – and we sat in the manager's office. He told us that the government had sequestrated our funds because we were part of the NUM. But we argued that we weren't part of the NUM.

HYWEL FRANCIS

The manager had just got back from holiday so he was hit with us demanding our money – now. We told him that it was our money – it was about £5,000 and it belonged to the support group, which had nothing to do with the NUM, and we wanted it all there and then, this morning; that what had been done was illegal and [that] we would hold him personally responsible.

SÎAN JAMES

We demanded he free it up. We made a cogent argument that it wasn't the union's money: we had divorced ourselves from the lodge. Poor man: both his brothers were miners and out on strike – so he didn't stand much chance.

HYWEL FRANCIS

We told the manager we were going off for a coffee and [that] when we got back, we wanted our money. When we reconvened, he said he had good news – that we could have our money – but [that he] wasn't 'absolutely sure' about when. We insisted that we wanted the money that moment, on the table in front of us. And, within the hour, it was: piles of notes and coins. And then I thought, 'What am I going to do now? I've got all this money – where am I going to put it?'

We decided we would give some of it to the bakery, some of it to the local food store and the rest of it was handed to me to hide. And a friend got me a black safety deposit box in a bank in another village, and that's where we put the money.

CHRISTINE POWELL

After that, we dealt in cash as much as we could. Every Sunday night, after the support group meeting, Stuart and I would sit in our back bedroom, counting out the money that had come in. We tipped everything out on the floor and we sat there, physically counting it all up. I ended up having £35,000 in cash in the house: we kept it in the drawer underneath the spare bed, and our dog – we had a Staffordshire bull terrier – slept on the bed. So that was our security.

At that time, we had a bank branch in the village, which opened on a Tuesday and Thursday morning. So every Tuesday, Stuart bagged it all up and dragged it up the road to the bank. That money was vital: we couldn't have fed a thousand people without it.

Throughout the summer, LGSM took the money from its bucket collections to the bank and posted regular cheques to the women running the support group in Dulais.

———

MARTIN GOODSELL

We sent the cheques to the Neath, Dulais and Swansea Valleys Miners Support Fund, rather than to the NUM, because this was the link we had formed and where the money was directly needed – and as there was always the risk of money sent to the NUM being sequestered.

———

Then, in early September, Dai Donovan told the support group he had invited LGSM to come to the valleys for a weekend.

———

DAI DONOVAN

It wasn't about wanting these gay and lesbian people to come down and have special treatment. I wanted them to come and see and be treated with the same courtesy as every other group which supported us. So I thought it was natural that they would come to South Wales and that they would be given the same welcome every other support group had been given.

CHRISTINE POWELL

When Dai said that they would like to come down and meet us, there was – again – stunned silence. There was a lot of homophobia here at the time. And it's down to lack of understanding and not having known gay people. It was an instinctive thing really; the way people had been brought up. There's an old saying here that 'in the valleys, men are men and women are glad.'

HYWEL FRANCIS

There were a couple of dozen people at the support-group meeting when Dai announced that he was going to bring a group of gays and lesbians down to the Dulais Valley the following week. Straight away there was a discussion about 'how do we deal with this situation? How do we handle this?' I asked, 'What do you mean?' Back came the answer, 'Well, we're going to have a dance and there will be people coming along to see two men dancing together. Of course, I'm not against it but it will mean peeping toms.'

SÎAN JAMES

One of the men came out with the classic comment, 'That will mean we have to watch men dancing together.' My response was that we had been watching women dancing together for years because that's what happens in clubs in Wales: all the women dance together while the men stand at the bar. So, to me, there was no difference, and it was about challenging those attitudes.

HYWEL FRANCIS

There wasn't open hostility – and certainly these people who put this forward weren't trying to be hostile. It was more a question of, 'Hang on a minute. Are you sure we should be doing this ?' and they were trying to couch it in a non-hostile way. I think it was a cultural thing really. The culture here was very definitely macho and people didn't talk about sexuality at all. Homosexuality was beyond their experience. Obviously, it existed in the valleys but not openly. It was certainly never discussed.

SÎAN JAMES

Anyway, the whole point of twinning with any group was that we would invite them down to see where their money was being spent.

HYWEL FRANCIS

But, as the minutes show, some people clearly weren't quite sure about the visit. In particular, an official of the lodge stood up and said, 'This hasn't been cleared with the union. These people are coming down here, they're coming to this event and it hasn't been discussed.' In the end, I neutralised it. I just told them the decision was done and they'd have to put up with it; to just get on with it. It was a question of, 'Don't worry about it – it's done. And this is important. These people in LGSM are making great sacrifices for us – they're raising a lot of money for us. We have to acknowledge the relationship and then build on it.' And so, very quickly, what resistance there was melted away.

DAI DONOVAN

But as I travelled back home, I had a fleeting thought: 'Will it be all right?' I just hoped that everything would be OK – and then I just dismissed it.

CHAPTER ELEVEN

DANCING IN DULAIS

The last weekend in October was set aside for LGSM to visit Dulais. As the date approached, there was trepidation – on both sides.

———

JAYNE FRANCIS-HEADON

My mam came home and said to me, 'There are lesbians and gays coming from London – what do you think of that, then?' My father was sitting in the chair when my mum announced this and he went, 'Oh, bloody hell. That's brilliant, isn't it? What the hell's going to happen to everybody around here? What's it going to be like when they're here?' My mam started laughing: she'd always been a really open-minded person and accepted anybody and everybody. Although at first she was a little bit apprehensive, she was also really excited; really animated by the prospect of the gays coming down here.

My own reaction was, 'What? Are they coming here? Are they going to stay here, in this house?' And when I told my friends, who were all my age, they were shocked. They didn't really know what to expect – as a teenager you have these pre-conceived ideas of what people might be like – and so they asked me, 'What will they do? What will they say? What will they be like?'

So I was apprehensive, anxious and excited all at the same time. I worried about how the village would react. I was worried about what everyone was going to think.

And I think they must have felt the same about us. They must have been apprehensive coming here to our community, meeting a bunch of miners, not knowing what to expect.

RAY GOODSPEED

When they gave us the invitation, we asked everyone, 'Who wants to come?' And, for me, it was – yes, absolutely! You couldn't have kept me away from that: it was marvellous and I really wanted to be there.

But I didn't know what to expect. I thought, 'Jesus, this is going to be interesting.' I'd only just arrived in London when I joined LGSM: I was this ingénue, this 'Thoroughly Modern Millie' type of person. I'd only told my parents I was gay less than a year ago – now I was going to a mining village as an open homosexual.

NICOLA FIELD

I never went to Dulais. The reason is that I was still very much affected by the rejection by my family and I was incredibly shy. Even though I was in LGSM and enjoyed being part of the group, I still had a sense of not belonging. I was socially anorexic. I was very scared of being abused and needed to be in familiar surroundings. I was scared of going to the mining communities. I was scared of being among straight people who might reject me.

BRETT HARAN

We had met Dai when he came up to London, and he was absolutely wonderful: he had an empathy about him. He assured us that it would be absolutely fine. But even so, although I remember being super-excited, I also felt a certain amount of anxiety over what the response would be like. A lot of us had thoughts like, 'What kind of reception will we get? Will the people there feel awkward about us staying?'

DAI DONOVAN

For anyone thinking it was remarkable that we had gay people coming down here, well, what was remarkable to me was that we had communities from three different valleys here and *they* were talking to one another. Because people from the Swansea Valley consider people from the Dulais Valley to be *'pobl o'r ochr arall'* – people from 'the other side'. And that co-operation between people who, without the support group, would have had no contact shows how far the strike was breaking down previous social barriers.

RAY GOODSPEED

We weren't the only group they invited down – loads of other groups who were supporting them had been invited to go there. But inviting us was a much bigger deal than inviting a trade-union group, just because of who – and what – we were.

MIKE JACKSON

They wanted to treat us like any other group. And those people who were uncomfortable about the whole thing were advised to stay away from our visit. You know: 'if you're going to make trouble, you'll get trouble back' sort of thing.

DAVE LEWIS

I was still a bit anxious about going. I was an urban dweller. I'd grown up in London and the idea of going to a close-knit community – any close-knit community – where everyone knew everyone else terrified me. And I think I was partly frightened in case the people there didn't live up to the image I had in my own mind of what a heroic struggle they were engaging in. I was a bit worried that I would be disappointed.

––––

Hovering in the background was the growing spectre of AIDS and the public perception of gay men as carriers of a deadly disease which threatened the entire population. Just a month earlier, the Conservative Town Council in Rugby had denounced all homosexuals as 'vile and perverted people' and declared that, unless it removed protection for gays from its employment policies, 'we shall give the people of Rugby the idea that this council welcomes queers and perverts.' The *Sun* promptly congratulated the council, proclaiming that it was time to stop the 'sick nonsense' of gay rights: 'Let's ALL follow Rugby in fighting back.'

———

CHRISTINE POWELL

The media was beginning to pile in on AIDS and I think a lot of people were frightened – you know: that thing about catching it if you shook hands with a gay person. That was the sort of rubbish which was going around.

SÎAN JAMES

I remember one of my neighbours saying that she was going to report us to the council because we were all going to get AIDS. And the whole village turned round and told her to piss off and not to talk such a load of rubbish. But really what that person wanted was reassurance. She needed us to tell her it was OK, and to tell her to come up the pub and meet some of the women and come and see what they are like.

———

By that October, there were more than a hundred recorded cases of AIDS in Britain, and forty-four men had died from the disease. For others who had been diagnosed as having the virus, living with what appeared to be a death sentence was often an isolating experience.

JONATHAN BLAKE

At the time, I was completely tied up with HIV and the diagnosis I'd had. I suppose I compartmentalised everything. I did tell people in LGSM about my diagnosis. I was out to them about this, even though I hadn't told my parents. But I didn't plan on telling anyone in Dulais: I think I felt that it was important to me but it wouldn't be important to them.

What *was* important was to be supportive of them, and help them get through what they were going through. It wasn't that I was protecting myself from any possible reaction from them; it was just about being supportive of them. The important thing was dealing with their immediate needs and what we could do to help.

——

On the afternoon of Friday, 26 October 1984, three mini-buses set off from London, carrying twenty-seven members of LGSM to Onllwyn in the heart of the Dulais Valley. It would turn into an eventful journey.

——

JONATHAN BLAKE

There was a huge group of us on the first visit. There were two Hackney Community Transport buses and a beat-up old Volkswagen as well: so quite a posse of us.

RAY GOODSPEED

Lord knows how we got the mini-buses to go there. They were real old crates. On the way down, we were going down the motorway, leaning out of the windows and blowing kisses at soldiers we passed en route.

JONATHAN BLAKE

I'd been to Wales – to Swansea and Neath – before, so I knew Wales a bit. But there's Wales and Wales, and the valleys are different. On the journey itself, there was that sense of adventure, but there was also this sinking feeling – you're not actually going to say anything, but you're thinking, 'What the fuck are we doing here?'

Because this was unknown territory: the people in the valleys could have been a whole lot of screaming homophobes and they didn't know what they were getting into.

RAY GOODSPEED

One of the mini-buses was pulled over by the police as we got into Wales. And we were thinking 'Oh God, we aren't going to be allowed to get to Dulais, and the mini-bus will be impounded.' But the policeman was a local guy and, after he gave us a quick look over, he gave us a nod and a wink – sort of 'nudge, nudge – my dad's a miner, now off you go.'

But Onllwyn was not an easy place to get to. Really, it's up all these little back lanes on the edge of the Brecon Beacons in the middle of nowhere.

GETHIN ROBERTS

Getting there was a nightmare. In those days, there was no sat-nav, no mobile phones and not much in the way of even phone boxes. It all went relatively OK until we got just near to the turn-off for the Dulais Valley – and at that point we got completely and utterly lost. We spent hours driving around getting more and more lost.

JONATHAN BLAKE

Because we got so lost, we didn't arrive till around one in the morning. By which time everything was sort of closed down.

RAY GOODSPEED

That's how we ended up sleeping the first night on Dai's floor, because we couldn't go to the families we were meant to be staying with. It was quite a big floor but, nevertheless, there were a lot of us camping out on it that night.

DAI DONOVAN

My house was an old cottage with the front two rooms knocked together to form a big living room. And they just slept all over the floor – and I mean *literally* all over the floor. I had two sheep dogs, a son of four and a daughter aged six. My daughter came down stairs in the morning – she'd been in bed when LGSM arrived – and the dogs bounded down with her all over the people in these sleeping bags. She was very prim and proper at that time and the look on her face was [of] 'What on earth is going on?' I never discussed it with her but what I ascribed to her reaction was the impropriety of it all.

———

The next morning, the twenty-seven gay activists were ferried across the valleys to meet the families who would look after them for the rest of the weekend.

———

CHRISTINE POWELL

When they came, Dai dropped three of them off to stay with us in our house. I was trying to be super cool about everything when one of them suddenly asked, 'Well, how do you feel about a bunch of queers coming down to see you then?' And that broke the ice.

―――

But in the miners' houses, LGSM came face to face with the realities of the strike in the Dulais Valley.

―――

BRETT HARAN

Money was tight, benefits were being cut and it was difficult for families to put food on the table. There was a nagging worry that the Tories might just starve the miners back to work. It was very much a war of attrition.

The family Martin and I stayed with had had a pet rabbit, which went in the pot (though they told their children it had escaped into the hills). That sounds made up but that's what things were like.

But still, there was this great sense of resolve and dignity in those mining communities. These were profoundly dignified people who were determined not to be trashed and not to be laid low – and not to be portrayed as the enemy within.

―――

The first hurdle faced by both the young gay activists and their more traditional hosts was not homosexuality, but diet.

―――

RAY GOODSPEED

We knew we would be staying with local families. They were all miners and their wives, and so we ate what they ate. Tins of corned beef, stew, that sort of thing.

On the way down, there had been a debate about whether, if you were vegetarian, it was OK to say to a miner giving you his last tin of corned beef that you couldn't eat it because you were vegetarian.

CHRISTINE POWELL

They told me that they were vegetarian, and I thought, 'You may be gay and I can handle that, but what the heck do I do with a vegetarian?'

RAY GOODSPEED

I wasn't veggie but, for the lesbians especially, there was this feeling that, if you were a lesbian, you should be a vegetarian. I didn't understand it then and I don't understand it now. Some of those who were just shut up and ate the corned beef; others did say, 'No, could I have something else, please?'

CHRISTINE POWELL

Eventually, I asked, 'Do you eat egg and chips?' And, thankfully, they did – because that's all I could manage.

——

But the biggest test was still ahead. On Saturday night, the young London gay activists were due to meet the miners and their families in the very traditional heart of the community.

——

JAYNE FRANCIS-HEADON

Saturday nights were the nights everyone went to the miners' welfare. Always, every week, without fail. The Onllwyn miners' welfare was a grey stone building: very square, very angular. In the front was the foyer and you went from there through the big double doors into the main hall – a big square room with fitted bench seats, a semi-circular bar and a full stage. The bar would be jam-packed on a Friday and Saturday. You could only get about a hundred and fifty people in there but – especially if the Onllwyn choir was performing there – it would be solid. Local bands would play for dances, but they didn't do the pop hits of the day. It was more old style: waltzes, that kind of thing.

It was very rugby and pony-club orientated. The walls were covered with photos of the local rugby players and their caps for Wales. And next to them were pony-club photographs and rosettes.

CHRISTINE POWELL

The club was packed that night. I don't think there was any antagonism: I think the atmosphere was 99 per cent curiosity. I mean, these people were from London. They were different. People here didn't think they had ever met a gay.

———

But for LGSM, the emotions were more complex – and more fearful. The evening would either be disastrous or would set the seal on a lasting friendship.

———

GETHIN ROBERTS

I was feeling tense. I think all of us felt very tense. I was nervous about how people were going to react. Is it going to be embarrassing and uncomfortable? I was expecting some awkwardness – not hostility, but I worried that both the local community and us would find the encounter awkward.

DAVE LEWIS

I was a bit frightened. Not that we'd get a bad reception but that the atmosphere would be cool and that they wouldn't know how to relate to us.

GETHIN ROBERTS

I perhaps had more idea what to expect than the others in LGSM. As well as growing up in North Wales, I'd also lived for a time in South Wales. For others, it would have been completely different to anything they'd ever seen before.

RAY GOODSPEED

I'd lived in Newcastle and had regularly drunk in working-men's clubs up there. So the general atmosphere and culture of working-men's clubs wasn't strange to me, but I'd never before walked through the door of one as a screaming queen. That was the X Factor; that was the difference.

GETHIN ROBERTS

To be honest, Onllwyn is isolated – and very geographically different to Islington or east London. Most people in LGSM would have never previously met a miner, and the people in Dulais would never have met a group of gay men and women before. They might have known an individual gay person, though they would never have talked about it, or if it was [talked about,] it would have been joked about. We had come to Onllwyn as a gay organisation so that was different and new and that's what we were worried about.

———

As the young activists walked up to the great double doors of the Onllwyn welfare hall, they were acutely conscious that not only did they come from a radically diverse culture but they looked very different to the people of the South Wales valleys.

———

PAUL CANNING

We might as well have come from Mars because we looked so different. We were the version of what was trendy in London. There was a big thing for retro American 1950s clothing back then. And that was the look. And we had buzzcuts. The miners didn't have buzzcuts so, physically, we just looked like different tribes.

RAY GOODSPEED

One of the other LGSM members had an enormous red Mohican and I thought, 'God, what's he going to do? He can't go there like that?' So there was this tension about how much we should 'behave'. How much should we rein it in a bit?

JONATHAN BLAKE

I remember that there was this real sense of trepidation. So much so that I don't actually remember walking in. But Mike says that there was this awful silence as the door opened and you just think, 'Shit, we shouldn't be here.'

CHRISTINE POWELL

I remember to this day seeing them all for the first time because they looked so different. I mean, this was 1984 in the valleys and in come these guys with chopped, cropped hair and Crombie coats – they just looked so different to the men round here.

JAYNE FRANCIS-HEADON

Their clothing was far better than anything we'd ever experienced. I mean, pretty much everybody dressed the same in our mining villages – the same jeans, the same top, the same jacket: everybody was very stereotypical; everybody looked the same.

JONATHAN BLAKE

But then somebody applauded and it was extraordinary. We were welcomed with such warmth and such generosity: really welcomed. And from there, it was bingo and dancing all the way.

CHRISTINE POWELL

We had a local comedian who got up and did a turn and he was very much a typical 'northern club comedian'. And within ten minutes, he'd managed to insult everybody in the room. A couple of people were getting quite upset about it until Hefina stood up and said, 'Nah – they've handled worse than that.'

GETHIN ROBERTS

As things turned out, it was neither embarrassing nor uncomfortable. The tension disappeared almost immediately –

as soon as we got to the bar and people started buying each other drinks.

SÎAN JAMES

Then one of the guys in the village, who was a bit of a hothead, turned to one the LGSM boys and said, 'I suppose you're "one of them". I can tell you're one of them.' And the LGSM guy said, 'One of them what?' And I thought it was all going to go off: we hadn't had anything like that but now I was thinking, 'Oh my God…'

And then the hothead said, 'One of them fucking teachers: I've had enough of fucking teachers.' And that was it: laughter.

———

But the laughter came more easily for the women than the men in Onllwyn miners' welfare hall that evening.

———

HYWEL FRANCIS

The real relationship wasn't with the miners. The real relationship was between the gays and the women of these valleys. And as LGSM said to me, 'Our biggest problem has always been with heterosexual men.'

DAVE LEWIS

We definitely got a different response to us from the women than we did from the men. The women were definitely more forthcoming. The men were a little bit more reticent. They weren't standoffish, but the women were much more confident about talking to us and asking us about ourselves.

JAYNE FRANCIS-HEADON

It was very traditional here: everybody expected a man to be with a woman, and that was the way things were. It was a very macho culture. If you looked at a group of miners, they'd all be men, they'd all have wives and children, and that's how it had been for their mothers and fathers before them, and their mothers and fathers before them, and so on.

For the men, there was definitely a bit of homophobia: it was lack of understanding really, because they'd never actually met an openly gay man and homosexuality would have been different and a bit frightening to them. But women see gay men differently to the way straight men do, don't they?

BRETT HARAN

The men had probably never been in the company of open and confident young gay people. So there was that sense that they didn't know how to relate to us because they'd never been in that situation before. It was easier for the women, I think: we didn't present as much of a threat.

SÎAN JAMES

It was the first time we'd had a relationship with men where it was perfectly acceptable to be sitting in those situations with them, and to be very affectionate, and not think that there was anything wrong with it. You would see people showing affection very openly. I don't mean sexual affection, just hugging and kissing. And in the valleys we just didn't do those sorts of things. Only with our family and behind closed doors. We were always very affectionate with our parents, for example: holding hands or hugging them. But not outside the family, not even with close friends – why would you think about doing that? It just wasn't done in the communities we were raised in. Someone flinging their arms around you: that would have been seen as soppy. People would have said, 'Oh, don't be so soppy, don't be silly.'

Suddenly we were seeing people who were very demonstrative and who had a different lifestyle – a different experience more than anything. It was very liberating.

JAYNE FRANCIS-HEADON

It was like the women were stronger than the men. So the women were the ones to take charge. That was the attitude: the women were very welcoming; that they had food and a drink and everyone was talking to each other. No one was left unspoken to: that's what the women did. They were like little beavers, making sure everybody was all right.

SÎAN JAMES

Friendships were made very, very quickly. We asked them about where they were from, why they wanted to be involved and what had made them support the miners. And that's when we started to realise that they had the same core values, and their sexuality and their lifestyle weren't the things that connected us.

CHRISTINE POWELL

The conversation that night was all about the strike. I mean, you weren't going to ask somebody, 'What's it like to be gay then?' You wouldn't expect to be asked, 'What's it like to be straight?' would you? And so it was like with any other group that had come down: we talked about the strike and we slagged off Thatcher.

DAVE LEWIS

I didn't talk to anyone about sexuality, or even politics: I didn't want to be thrusting my opinions down the throats of people that were living it day in and day out. And so I let them dictate the discussions and we only really talked about the strike.

PAUL CANNING

We talked about politics. I don't remember them asking me about life as a gay man in London. But it wasn't the sort of thing that you talked about generally. I mean, no one wanted to talk about it in Coalville. It's kind of a British reserve thing: you just don't talk about difficult subjects. And, obviously, that was a big 'staring you in the face, oh my God' difficult subject. So we didn't talk about sex, though there was some interest from some of the women. I think that came from them being kind of boxed in. I mean, they were working-class women, housewives – that was their role. So, in a sense, we represented a kind of freedom from that.

SÎAN JAMES

It was quite exciting to meet other people who thought like we did but who also encouraged us to think in a different way. And what we discovered was that we were far more alike than we were different. And it didn't really matter where they were from or what their background and experiences were. They believed in the same things that we believed in.

——

For some, though, the curiosity about gay men's lives was too strong to resist completely.

——

RAY GOODSPEED

People in the village were trying to make us feel welcome and make us feel like a normal group of visitors. But they were also asking about the gay scene and when I first knew I was gay, and what did my mother think?

And someone did ask one of the gay couples which one did the housework. You know: 'How does that work – who's the husband and who's the wife?' sort of thing. It wasn't hostile; it was just curiosity. There was a lot of curiosity.

DAI DONOVAN

I've heard that some people said to them, 'Well, who's the wife and who's the husband?' Well, if somebody had said that near me, I'd have fucking clipped them around the ear.

HYWEL FRANCIS

The political point of the link between LGSM and this valley was that we should acknowledge and build alliances of groups of people who had been – or were being – besieged. It was a common cause between miners and gays. They – the gays – had horrendous problems compared with us, and it was vital to acknowledge with gratitude what they were doing for us, and build the relationship so we could understand each other's communities.

JAYNE FRANCIS-HEADON

We talked about their struggles and what they'd been through with Thatcherism and all of the discrimination they'd suffered. Mark Ashton took me under his wing: he always had loads to say, so I didn't really get to say much. But I did want to ask about their lives as gay men, how they lived and what they did in London.

I found it sad that many of them had had to leave where they originally came from and go to London because that was the only place they could really be free. And I understood that they found a community there that they could be part of and feel safe in.

———

By the end of the evening, the fears which had preyed on the minds of both the villagers and the young gay activists had been dissolved by alcohol – and by the discovery of a common cause against a shared enemy.

———

MIKE JACKSON

What was so wonderful for me on that very first visit was that all these people knew about us was that we were lesbians and gay men, and we supported them in their strike. All I ever wanted was acceptance, and here it was, in bucketloads, in this Welsh miners' welfare club.

DAVE LEWIS

I saw a world that I had never ever had any image of. This frightening world where everyone knew everyone, and most were involved in mining in one way or another. I wasn't expecting them to be as cultured, as outward looking and as aware as I found them. Because they *were* aware of the outside world: they were happy in theirs but they had developed an awareness that I, in my bigoted mind, hadn't credited them with before I arrived.

RAY GOODSPEED

Afterwards, as Dave Lewis and I went back to the caravan in which we were staying, I remember clearly turning to him and saying, 'Jesus, what are we doing? This is incredible. What are we doing here? What the hell?' And it was very, very moving.

––––

But the increasingly harsh realities – of the lack of money in the valleys, and of the fear of increasing police attention – were brought home later that night.

––––

CHRISTINE POWELL

At some point during that Saturday night, the radio was

pinched out of LGSM's mini-bus. And, obviously, they were concerned because it was a hired vehicle. So we phoned the police on Sunday morning and quite a lot of police turned up, and really quickly.

Now, normally, if you phoned the police to report someone pinching the radio out of a van, they would take a good while to come out – in fact, they would usually have dealt with that sort of thing by giving a crime number out over the phone. Why did so many of them come out so quickly? I'm not a paranoid person but I know that my phone was tapped at the time: there were clicks and buzzes and whirrs on the line, and I realised that the police knew all that was going on. It was obvious that they knew who we had staying with us – Lesbians and Gays Support the Miners – with 'support the miners' being the most crucial part of that.

———

The next day, Dai Donovan took the LGSM members to see what exactly it was that the miners were fighting for.

———

DAI DONOVAN

To my mind, the important reason to bring them to Dulais was *not* to take them to the welfare hall and entertain them but to take them to the collieries and show them the lack of investment in the industry over many decades. So I arranged a visit to the collieries at Blaenant and Treforgan.

BRETT HARAN

I thought we were going to be shown around a typical mining

village and go down a pit. And we did go to one – a drift mine at Treforgan. I hadn't had any romantic notions about what coal mining was like: I knew it was a grimy, gritty, unpleasant job. But when we walked into it, my reaction was, 'God, people actually work in these conditions.'

As the mini-buses made their way out of the Dulais Valley on the Sunday evening, the twenty-seven LGSM members inside were filled with a profound respect for the women and men of the South Wales coalfield, and a renewed determination to support their struggle against the forces trying to starve them into submission.

JONATHAN BLAKE

We were welcomed by these people who were literally starving. They were being battered by the State – the full force of the State was coming down on them.

The way they were being treated was just awful. We were there for a long weekend, and that they could offer such hospitality was amazing – really amazing.

GETHIN ROBERTS

On the surface, it seemed as though people in the community were having a good time; were still able to have a good time and buy each other drinks. But as we got to talk to them and find out more about the reality of their lives, it became clear that they were largely dependent on food parcels and that many of them were building up massive rent or mortgage arrears. They were having to borrow money right, left and centre. The only thing between them and starvation was support from people like us and trades unions. And there was a recognition that, while we were with them, we were eating their food, and there was a kind of feeling [of] 'Oh, I shouldn't have a second sausage.'

MIKE JACKSON

I think the visit made everyone very keen not to mess around but to get on with the job. We were on the gay scene in London and, when we went to Wales, we saw what it was like for them and heard the stories of their lives: it made us all more determined when we got back to London to do our best for them.

GETHIN ROBERTS

It would be too dramatic to say that the visit changed me. But it did make me feel that bit more committed to helping.

Once you could put a face and a name to people – to families and kids who had become your friends – it became much more important; much less abstract. Before we went down, I felt I was doing the collections to support other workers and fellow trade unionists. Once we had met these people, it became much more personal. The money in my bucket on a collection outside a gay pub in London would feed a family I knew in Dulais for a day or so.

———

As the winter of 1984 deepened, those bucket collections would be needed more than ever before. The strike was entering its eighth month, Christmas was looming and the valleys were beginning to wonder how long their families could hold out.

CHAPTER TWELVE
PITS AND PERVERTS

On 23 October 1984 all the NUM's assets were seized, by court order. It was the culmination of months of concerted legal attacks on the union and its leadership.

The battle had begun in September when working miners from Derbyshire and Nottinghamshire asked the High Court in London to rule that the strike was illegal because no national ballot had been held. The judge, Mr Justice Nicholls, declined to order the NUM to hold a ballot but he issued an injunction, forbidding the union from disciplining its members who crossed picket lines. On 28 September – the day the court made its ruling – Arthur Scargill struck a defiant note in a television interview: 'There is no high court judge going to take away the democratic right to deal with internal affairs. We are an independent democratic union.'

The High Court viewed this as contempt of court. It gave the miners' leader five days to reconsider. Scargill refused to do so.

'If the choice is to spend a term in Pentonville or any other prison or to live by the imprisonment of my mind for betraying my class, the choice is that I stand by my class and my union.'[9]

On 10 October – in a move backed even by traditional Labour newspapers – the High Court fined Scargill £1,000 and the NUM £200,000. Thirteen days later, all of the union's assets were seized. The immediate effect was to cut off the very meagre expenses payments to NUM pickets. In turn, this would put the coalfield communities under even greater financial strain.

DAI DONOVAN

We had received £9 a day from the union if you went out picketing but that was to pay for food and the petrol to get you there. Sequestration meant the NUM couldn't pay this. And I think picketing was important. It gave people a stake in the strike. If they had been sitting at home, exposed to the constant stream of hostile news, it would have been bad for morale.

In November 1984 national newspapers reported that mining communities were receiving funds from the Kremlin. Although the money had, in reality, been raised by donations from miners across the Soviet Union to ease the growing hardship throughout British coalfields, it was portrayed as further evidence of the threat posed by the strikers to Britain.

------

[9] Quoted in the *Financial Times*, 5 October 1984.

CHRISTINE POWELL

We didn't get much positive press coverage. The media was on Thatcher's side in the miner's strike. Throughout the strike, we brought miners and their families down to South Wales from the Leicestershire and Nottinghamshire coalfields, which were having a really rough time, so they could have a break – a bit of a breather. We paid for them to come down to us. Of course, you never hear about this. According to the press, the mining communities weren't supposed to be nice people in any way shape or form – we were the enemy within.

———

The same month, on a trip to Moscow, Labour leader Neil Kinnock denied Russian press reports that British miners were being starved into submission: 'I told them that while people were enduring very great hardship there was no hunger, and that the reports of deprivation on that scale were somewhat misleading.'[10]

Despite Kinnock's claims, in the South Wales valleys the reality was of a community beginning to struggle for survival. As winter deepened, families found it increasingly difficult to heat their homes.

———

SÎAN JAMES

Like most people, our heating in the house was coal fired, and all miners had got an allowance from their colliery.

———

[10] Quoted in the *Yorkshire Post*, 24 November 1984.

JAYNE FRANCIS-HEADON

Everyone who worked at the pit got an allowance of coal. It was deducted from the men's wages but it was an entitlement. Every house had a coal shed and that's where the coal was delivered, ready to be broken up to heat their houses and their water. There was no central heating and everyone had coal fires. Coal was the lifeblood of our community.

CHRISTINE POWELL

You got seven loads of what was called 'concessionary coal' per year, tipped outside the house. It was part of a pay agreement so it was free in the sense that we didn't pay for it but it formed part of the men's wages. For most people, that was their only means of heating the house, heating the water and cooking.

SÎAN JAMES

But because Martin was on strike, that was cut off. We only got one delivery during the entire strike. So we raided coal. We women used to go up to the old washery and steal bits of coal.

JAYNE FRANCIS-HEADON

Some of the younger boys in the villages would go out at night up on to the tips and slag heaps to bring down as much coal as they could possibly get. It was a dangerous job: they had to run the gauntlet of security guards and police.

SÎAN JAMES

One night, Hefina got an old pram and we set off to fill it up with coal from the washery. We got there but, after we'd filled this pram, we heard someone coming so we nipped round the corner to hide, leaving the pram – full of coal – where it was. When whoever it was had passed by, we went back out and found that some bastard had nicked the pram and the coal. So that was the end of that night's adventure.

But that was an exception. Ours was a community where we helped each other and shared things. There was a tradition here that, when somebody had a baby, you'd go and leave coal on their doorstep. And the farmers in our end of the valley allowed us to cut wood. So our support group bought chainsaws and went up to the woods during the day, cut down old trees and sawed them up into logs. Then it would be taken round and shared throughout the community – especially the old age pensioners. That wood really kept us going.

——

In London, LGSM members continued their bucket collections to raise funds for the Neath, Dulais and Upper Swansea Valley Support Group. But they also invited the families who had looked after them to see first hand what life was like for gay men and women in the capital.

——

SÎAN JAMES

We went up to London several times after the first visit, staying with people who had stayed with us. We had marvellous times up there.

We did all the clubs – Heaven, Stringfellows – we did them all. It was quite a change from a night out at the miners' welfare hall in Onllwyn. I mean, there were cross dressers and people had their alter egos. We were meeting people who were very artistic and flamboyant.

GETHIN ROBERTS

They were coming up to London and discovering new experiences. They were finding out about cannabis and casual sex, which hadn't really penetrated into the valleys – or at least not into respectable chapel-going families. A lot of the stuff we introduced them to was, I think, quite novel for them. Open relationships, recreational drug use. Hefina, for example, would not previously have been exposed to the gay scene and she certainly wouldn't have known anyone who smoked a joint: no one would have smoked a joint in her house before the strike.

SÎAN JAMES

I remember going to an all-nighter and coming out at six o' clock in the morning and there had been lots of noise and dancing and I was wondering how the LGSM people handled it. So I turned to Gethin and said, 'Is this what you do all the time?' And he said, 'No, we bloody don't – we only do this when you lot are up here.'

JAYNE FRANCIS-HEADON

One night, we went off to Heaven nightclub and, of course, there were gay men everywhere.

But we liked them: they were non-threatening. Some of them were quite feminine and they were just the loveliest men that we had ever met. Compared to the village boys – the macho village boys – these were really caring men who wanted to listen to you and were really friendly. I felt really safe with them. I always felt safe with the LGSM guys.

And then I went to the toilet and – wow: there were women having sex in the toilet, very loudly with the cubicle doors open. So I ran out of there: I was really frightened. I was just a sixteen-year-old little girl from the Welsh valleys.

When they came to us in Dulais, I hadn't talked to them about what being gay actually involved. But when I went to London, I did. I think I had to go into their community to see how they lived and what they did before I asked them those questions.

SÎAN JAMES

Sometimes they would confide in us about aspects of their sexuality which were shocking. Pretty extreme things – especially in the height of the HIV scare. But the thing was that they trusted us to see it. They were trusting us with a very important part of themselves and, as the relationship between us all progressed, they wanted us to see that part of their lives. They didn't want to hide behind any falseness.

––––

But, as the relationship between the South Wales mining families and LGSM deepened, the Dulais support group was also exposed to the differing attitudes of gay men and lesbian women.

SÎAN JAMES

The lesbians were very determined to give us a real feminist perspective. We were going to just do the nightclubbing – which we loved – while they were determined that we were going to see things from that feminist perspective. And again, most of us had never had that experience before.

WENDY CALDON

It wasn't a question of showing them something to open their eyes. I think the women's eyes were more open than ours were. One day, we came back to Kentish Town Women's Centre and did badge making and relaxation and talking and there was a crèche. Jayne Francis-Headon – Hefina's daughter – said that day had really influenced them all: they'd never had time and space before for a women's get together.

JAYNE FRANCIS-HEADON

I attended a women's day they had organised. That was the first time I'd met a whole load of lesbians all together and, to be honest, they struck me as the grumpiest people I'd ever come across. I didn't see one of them smile – all of them in that room seemed to have a real gripe with life and they were really angry. And I didn't like it; I didn't like being in that room with them.

WENDY CALDON

Being in LAPC was not all mung beans and consciousness-raising. We might have talked to them about feminism but that [day] was about feminism in action, just women getting together and talking about stuff and relaxing. There were also many really fun times, including a benefit gig we put on at The Bell in Kings Cross. I can't stand being talked at and hectored at, and I think that can be more effective. But sometimes the sheer stress of fighting sexism, homophobia and anti-feminism was – and still is – exhausting, so feelings can get intense. We were very committed to the cause of supporting the strike and I'm really proud of that.

CHRISTINE POWELL

I hate to say it but the girls kind of scared me a bit. They seemed to me to be trying to be so hard and I thought, 'I don't know how to cope with this.'

JAYNE FRANCIS-HEADON

But we did bring back ideas from our visits there. After Lesbians Against Pit Closures put on a women's day, we organised some women's days in our communities. So we went from tunnel vision into a sense of the world opening up to us. But, politically, it was too much for me. Heavy stuff, all about empowering women, and talks about CND and human rights and things like that. And it was all 'women, women, women and men shouldn't exist' kind of thing. I didn't understand at the time why they were so cross all the time. I absolutely never got that sense of anger from the gay men, so I didn't understand it or see why it was necessary.

———

For at least one of the lesbians, this sense of discomfort was something she had come to expect.

STEPHANIE CHAMBERS

I had noticed in Wales that both the men and the women found it easier to relate to, and speak with, gay men than the lesbians. They could cope with the gay boys and they could have professional relationships with the gay men of LGSM. But the gay ladies? That was hard. Lesbians weren't part of the big gang.

I remember being at a social evening at the miners' club. I noticed a few young men were dinking at the bar. I held my glass up in a 'cheers' gesture to them. They looked at me and turned around to face the bar. Having said that, the majority of men and women welcomed me, as a lesbian, into their community.

———

This tension would soon emerge as the first real fault line within the unity of LGSM's efforts on behalf of the miners. But as it simmered, the activists immersed themselves in ever more flamboyant fund-raising events. Even a humble jumble sale was given the full LGSM treatment.

———

MIKE JACKSON

Because we'd been donated so much stuff – some of it quite good quality – we decided to hold a preview for it the night before the sale. We called it 'The Night of A Thousand Socks'. It was meant as a bit of PR and we publicised it in *Capital Gay* but it was such a queeny thing to do – a preview for a jumble sale, for God's sake! We all dressed up for it. I wore a fluorescent workman's jerkin, a blue frock that I'd made out of a polythene bag and a wig – hideous!

At that stage, LGSM was getting very popular within the gay community so the preview wasn't solely political: it involved quite a lot of flirting between LGSM core members and our developing fan club. And I think that's really important in politics because you've got to survive; you've got to live. Yes, this is really serious but let's have a fucking break.

It was in that spirit – a heady brew of politics and fun – that LGSM announced its most ambitious fund-raising event.

Capital Gay, 22 November 22 1984

'Top gay rock band Bronski Beat are topping the bill of a major benefit night being organised by the Lesbians and Gays Support the Miners group at The Electric Ballroom, Camden, next month.'

MIKE JACKSON

Mark Ashton and Jimmy Somerville, the singer in Bronski Beat, were good mates. They'd both ended up in London at roughly the same time – Jimmy from a rough Glaswegian background, Mark from Portrush in Northern Ireland. They just hit it off and were like the Terrible Twins, going round terrorising London.

And then Jimmy was discovered – his voice was discovered – and he started on a fast trajectory to fame round about the same time as LGSM started. So it was quite natural to get Jimmy and Bronski Beat to headline. We knew we'd got that resource because we knew Jimmy would be sympathetic.

CAPITAL GAY, 22 NOVEMBER 1984

'The group says: 'All lesbian and gay organisations are asked to show their solidarity by bringing their banners to the ball, or staffing stalls on behalf of their respective organisations.'

MIKE JACKSON

All the miners support groups were trying to think of different ways to raise money. This concert was just an extension of our bucket-collecting activities. But it was announced in *NME* – and that was a huge fillip to the marketing.

———

The benefit gig was scheduled for 10 December but, before posters for the event could be designed and printed, a suitably provocative title was needed. The choice – 'Pits and Perverts' – neatly encapsulated the political alliance between miners and gays but it also nodded knowingly to the hostility of the tabloid press to both groups.

———

COLIN CLEWS

No one is quite sure where the title came from. Originally, it was thought to derive from a newspaper headline but it now seems more likely that it was merely a parody of tabloid representations of lesbians and gay men.

RAY GOODSPEED

The urban myth is that the title 'Pits and Perverts' came from a headline in the *Sun*. But that's just not true.

COLIN CLEWS

As with the word 'queer', 'perverts' was a term that was originally meant to injure but was used instead as a symbol of defiance and unity in the face of Margaret Thatcher's powerful press-baron friends.

———

On the afternoon of the gig, the Neath, Dulais and Upper Swansea Valley Support Group chartered a mini-bus and set out along the M4 towards London.

———

SÎAN JAMES

Somebody rang somebody to tell LGSM we were on the way. This was a time before mobile phones, so the call had been made from a phone box at the services. And we were told that, when we got to London, we were to make our way to The Fallen Angel pub in Islington and that there would be a vegetarian meal awaiting us there. Well, everybody panicked: absolute panic.

My dad had given us the money to go and everybody else had a little bit of money so we all pooled it, thinking, 'This is an emergency.' And so, when we parked the van up in Islington, we all went for fish and chips because we thought the vegetarian food would be horrible – stuff like mung beans and rice and that crap – and we'd end up starving.

JAYNE FRANCIS-HEADON

Food was a massive culture difference. There were a lot of them who were vegetarian. And when we went to their events, we

213

kind of dreaded what would be there to eat. Because there was no whole-hearted stodgy kind of food – it was all rice and beans and courgettes and salad. And I'd never experienced any of that before. I had no idea what it was and I didn't like the taste of it.

SÎAN JAMES

But when we got into The Fallen Angel, there was this massive spread laid out – all this beautiful food, all lovingly prepared. It really was beautiful – it didn't look like any vegetarian food we'd ever imagined. And we looked at each other and said, 'Shit – wish we hadn't eaten that fish and chips.' We felt terrible: all the LGSM people were trying to get us to eat and we were all full. So we had to admit what we'd done then.

––––

Bronksi Beat was then one of the biggest names in music, with three Top 20 singles in 1984 alone. At a time when major pop stars had to hide their sexuality, all its members were openly gay and their songs, which tackled homophobia and discrimination, were instrumental in breaking down anti-gay prejudice.

––––

MIKE JACKSON

I think a lot of people that night came to see Bronski Beat: perhaps people who weren't particularly committed to the miners' cause but were fans of the music.

––––

But gay or straight, pro- or anti-strike, the 1,500 people who crowded into The Electric Ballroom found themselves mingling with miners from all over Britain.

MIKE JACKSON

The protocol was that, when you had a benefit for the miners, striking miners got in free of charge. So on the night, there were regional accents from everywhere – Scotland, Yorkshire, Wales.

BRETT HARAN

I remember watching the acts and feeling this sense of elation that this thing was happening. We had a young Welsh miner and his girlfriend staying with us: he was so excited to be there when Jimmy Somerville was performing.

MIKE JACKSON

A young Scottish miner was there on his own. I had the Pits and Perverts T-shirt on and he asked me if I was anything to do with it. I said that I was one of the organisers. He was completely bemused by the whole thing. He said, 'I'd no idea that you supported us.' So I put my arm round his shoulder and gestured at the one and a half thousand people there and said, 'Well, now you do.'

———

Near the end of the evening, LGSM invited Dai Donovan on to the stage to address the crowd.

———

DAI DONOVAN

I think I was probably a bit boring. I'm not very musical so, if I can whistle to it, I certainly can't clap to it. Also, I was thirty-nine years of age so, while I was aware of Bronksi Beat and I knew that they were in the charts, I certainly can't say anything other than that they were important. I have only vague memories of my speech. I don't think I wrote anything down. I spoke from the heart. I'm not a particularly good speaker about just anything but, if I care about something – and I cared about this – I can be. And I believed in everything I said.

———

Dai Donovan's Speech at Pits and Perverts

You have worn our badge, 'Coal not Dole', and you know what harassment means, as we do. Now we will pin your badge on us; we will support you.

It won't change overnight, but now 140,000 miners know that there are other causes and other problems. We know about blacks and gays and nuclear disarmament, and we will never be the same.

At the end of the night, LGSM counted up the takings and discovered that the benefit had raised £5,650 – the equivalent of more than £20,000 today – for the striking miners and their families in the South Wales valleys. It also led to an immediate upsurge in other donations: but the Neath, Dulais and Upper Swansea Valley Support Group decided it could not keep all the money.

———

HYWEL FRANCIS

After the concert, £19,000 came into our support-group funds. But at that time, other areas were struggling: they hadn't raised the money their communities needed. They were desperate – really up against it – and the strike seemed likely to collapse there.

So our support group had a discussion and we said to ourselves, 'What's the point of all this money being in our accounts if the strike is going to collapse somewhere else?' So we gave £5,000 to one valley and £5,000 to another: we just shifted the money anywhere it was needed.

———

That December, money was tight all over the Welsh coalfield. The strike was now in its ninth month and the families in the Dulais Valley were facing a bleak midwinter.

———

JAYNE FRANCIS-HEADON

When Christmas approached that year, that's when we really struggled. As the winter months dragged on and we were still on strike, people found it difficult to pay their bills. My sister had a mortgage but, because her husband was on strike and there was no money coming in, they couldn't pay it, and she was pregnant as well. That's when we, as a family, really felt the hardship.

Our food was poor – stewed meat out of a tin and a few potatoes. On a daily basis, there was just whatever could be slopped up in front of us and none of us were getting enough to eat. Everybody was struggling: the food parcels were vital.

A bit of bread, a few potatoes, the tins of meat and a bit of fruit in each. That was it really. It was a treat if there was a tin of Carnation milk or a tin of peaches in there.

———

But the plight of miners' families was rarely discussed in newspapers or on television. That festive season, another appeal was made to the nation's conscience and pockets. Band Aid's 'Do They Know It's Christmas' shot to the top of the charts within days of its release and raised much-needed millions for anti-famine efforts in Ethiopia. But the well-publicised attitude of the project's founder, Bob Geldof, exasperated families across the South Wales coalfield.

'English pop music is highly politicized. Records come out in support of a strike, and they do not do very well. Let's take the coal-miners strike, which was viewed outside this country possibly as this great struggle, which it wasn't … eighty percent of the people didn't agree with the strike.'[11]

____

SÎAN JAMES

I still haven't forgiven people like that silly pop star, Bob Geldof, for saying, 'Don't give your money to the miners; give your money to Band Aid.' Hold on: it's not an either-or situation. It's a different struggle. We felt very, very strongly about that.

____

But Band Aid's deliberately apolitical stance delighted Prime Minister Margaret Thatcher. She told *Smash Hits* magazine, 'What fascinated me was that it was not "why doesn't the government give more?' but 'what can I do as a person?' That was Bob Geldof's approach.'

As with her attack on the miners as 'the enemy within', Mrs Thatcher conveniently overlooked the fact that the coalfield

____

[11] Bob Geldof interview in *Rolling Stone* magazine, 5 December 1985.

communities had long since adopted the same attributes of self-help that she so praised in Band Aid. Even as her government tightened the financial noose around the necks of the striking miners and their families, the Neath, Dulais and Upper Swansea Valley Support Group worked to ensure Christmas would be as normal as possible.

———

CHRISTINE POWELL

We were determined that every family would have a turkey – and we did that. And we said that every kid would have presents – and we did that. I've still got all our records, including the order we placed for Christmas presents for the kids in the villages.

———

But, despite their best efforts, the first cracks in the community's solidarity were beginning to show.

———

CHRISTINE POWELL

We did get some opposition. One of the postmen complained about having to deliver kids toys, which people sent to me for distribution, but another postman soon put him right about that.

And then my dad put a little advert in the paper asking for toys to be donated. One day, he got an envelope through the post and, when he opened it, he found that advert, cut up into pieces: that was all that was in there. Someone had taken the time to do that and to send it to him – with a first-class stamp as well.

———

Before long, those divisions would be forced out into the open throughout Britain's coalfields. And they would mirror a developing fault line within the gay community that was doing so much to support them.

CHAPTER THIRTEEN

DIVISIONS

At the beginning of 1985, homosexual men once again found themselves under attack by politicians and the press. In January the Chair of the House of Commons Health Committee, Conservative MP Jill Knight, demanded that AIDS be made a legally notifiable disease, and that new laws should be introduced which would allow sufferers to be forcibly detained in hospital.

It was the start of what would become a concerted campaign, intended to stigmatise and isolate gay men. But the young activists in LGSM were also facing internal argument and division.

WENDY CALDON

In January 1985 Nicola Field approached me and said some

of the women from LGSM were getting together a separate lesbians support group for the miners. I was absolutely up for that, and that's how Lesbians Against Pit Closures (LAPC) started.

––––

The formation of LAPC marked the re-emergence of the old fault line between gay men and lesbians – exacerbated by political tensions between the left-wing factions in the group – which had been felt by some of LGSM's women members almost from the start.

––––

NICOLA FIELD

When the strike started, I was generally a socialist but I was prioritising my lesbian and gay stuff. And one of my colleagues in our video group had been to an LGSM meeting and said that I should also go along.

I was a bit worried because I saw men as oppressive and was a bit scared that I wouldn't be able to argue with them or handle it politically. But I also knew that the miners had to be supported against Thatcher so I also went with all that fear that I'd be pilloried as a traitor to women by feminists. And I found it was a room full of men: there was only one other woman there. However, she was really helpful. She was a member of the Socialist Workers Party and I learned a lot from her. She came round to my flat in Deptford, showed me how to put together a collection bucket and petition sheet, and we went to my local gay pub. That's how I got started building solidarity.

STEPHANIE CHAMBERS

The first time I went to an LGSM meeting, my initial thought was, 'Oh, there's a lot of men here.' And it really was full of a lot of men. And when you get a lot of men in an enclosed room with the windows closed, it can get fairly smelly. I remember we had to sit on the floor and [I was] thinking, 'For God's sake, we're not at school.'

And there were a few men in LGSM who weren't comfortable in women's company and would have liked me to leave. But I just dug my heels in even more.

WENDY CALDON

I think I went to a couple of meetings and sat at the back a bit. At that time, I was still learning the various nuances of the left and it was difficult because Mark Ashton was a superstar – he had a real presence. And he would say something, then someone would come back at him and I didn't really understand it all. I knew it was very dynamic and people were taking positions and it was difficult to find my position in it.

NICOLA FIELD

LGSM had different left-wing groups who were represented. They found it very difficult to work together because of their differing political frameworks. And it was quite bullying, so that I saw men tearing into each other remorselessly on points of political theory at meetings. I could see that it was a very unforgiving environment and you would have to be completely unaligned and rise above it to cope with being there.

Because we met a lot of women in the clubs who wanted to support the miners but didn't want to work with men, we agreed to set up a separate lesbian group. And I knew where I was with that.

———

The formation of LAPC caused a rift within LGSM: some of the activists saw it as a factional split; others recognised the underlying tension it reflected.

———

DAVE LEWIS

I think it was a mistake. There was no need for it: we were all engaged in a huge war and I think that the war – support for the miners – was more important than how we, as individuals, might feel. It wasn't a consciousness-raising workshop we were involved with, and the women that were in LGSM were split pretty evenly. Perhaps even the majority were against the idea of LAPC splitting off.

STEPHANIE CHAMBERS

Personally, I thought it was divisive. I thought the lesbians were being divisive and I thought we needed as many people as possible in the group. LGSM wasn't about women's issues in the strike. It was about raising money and the miner's strike and supporting, in our case, Dulais. It wasn't about women's politics and how they were feeling. It was hard work. When people brought their own politics into the group – like the SWP tried to do – Mike Jackson stopped them and threw it back at them.

PAUL CANNING

I perfectly understood the split. Nobody within LGSM was interested in having a diverse group. We had flaming rows about this. For me, it was just blindingly obvious, because there were no black people in LGSM and no women.

And it struck me as the same principle. I don't think that the leadership of LGSM – because of their Leninism – saw this as important.

WENDY CALDON

LGSM meetings were quite large and could be quite intimidating. There were so many people with big opinions that there was a lot of shouting. Which is fine but it was a very male way of organising and I wanted to organise in a female way. I knew I wanted to do something; not just talk. I wanted to be involved; not just do the collecting.

COLIN CLEWS

My perception was that LGSM was solely about raising money for the miners. Nothing else. But the women did feel that there was a need to work with the women within the community, and to use the opportunity to educate them on women's issues. That was what lesbians saw that we couldn't do. I certainly wasn't opposed to that. As a gay man, I just had a different perspective.

NICOLA FIELD

At that time, lesbians organised separately, lesbians and gays wouldn't work with straights, and lesbians and gays generally didn't like bisexuals. And when I met people who wanted to form a lesbian-only support group, I thought, 'Well, this will just increase the number of people collecting money. The men can't come in the women's clubs and a lot of the women won't go to mixed events, so why not?'

DAVE LEWIS

It would have been quite possible for the women to do women-only collections at women-only venues. And, in fact, that had already been going on, right from the inception of the group. I think it was some of the women who weren't at all comfortable at working with men – period – following through on that philosophy.

―――

As well as collecting separately from LGSM, Lesbians Against Pit Closures also decided to form new links with the support group for a coalfield far away from South Wales.

―――

NICOLA FIELD

We twinned with a different community to LGSM. We twinned with Rhodesia mine in Nottinghamshire. We had meetings, we collected and we organised benefits.

WENDY CALDON

LAPC met every Monday at the Drill Hall in Gower Street, near the University of London. There were fifteen of us in the group but there were about eight or nine of us who were really committed. Some of the group were students so they collected during the day. Because I was working full time, I collected at the Drill Hall on a Monday night. We organised women-only benefits and raised a lot of money. We had bands on and a disco. It was all women and it was just jumping.

But the main thing was to collect money: that was absolutely it. We did really well. We were a small group but we managed to raise over £1,000.

NICOLA FIELD

But it was seen as a retrograde or unnecessary step by a lot of men in LGSM. To this day, there are some men in LGSM who disagree vehemently with it. Any idea that women might have found LGSM an untoward environment is something they reject.

DAVE LEWIS

The formation of LAPC wasn't the end of the world, by any stretch of the imagination, and I don't think it did any harm, but I think it was a shame. I think it was emblematic of some of the dead ends that the left drove up in the early 1980s. The left was going down a road of self-organisations – women-only, black-only. There's nothing intrinsically wrong with that but I've never been one for separating yourself from the perceived problem. If the perceived problem is sexism or racism, one ought to tackle that and take it on. And I don't think you do that if you split yourself off.

MIKE JACKSON

I didn't see the lesbians as being divisive. To my mind, if we wanted to have a group of lesbians and gay men supporting the miners autonomously of other political organisations, I didn't see how we could complain that lesbians wanted to form their own autonomous group to do the same. It was all the same principle.

STEPHANIE CHAMBERS

I do understand why they did it. I think they felt dominated by the men; that their voice wasn't being heard. But I didn't go to any LAPC meetings. I'm not even sure if they asked me but I wouldn't have gone even if they had. Other women still did go to the LGSM meetings. But I remember meetings where I was the only woman and it felt as if I was the lesbian in Lesbian and Gays Support the Miners.

———

Despite the hostility of some LGSM members to LAPC, the two organisations overcame their differences and found a way of co-operating. But, beneath the surface, the scars lingered.

———

WENDY CALDON

We organised joint things with LGSM and we went to the same clubs and pubs. The Fallen Angel had one night a week which was women only and, when they tried to stop that, some of the LGSM guys came and stood on the picket line we'd organised outside it. A lot of gay men at that time were extremely supportive of lesbian issues.

But there were others in LGSM who said – and still say – why did LAPC leave LGSM?

These people always praise the role of women – the miners' wives – during the strike, so why they find LAPC difficult is a bit beyond me. I know that solidarity and identity often clash in left-wing politics but identity and different experiences of oppression cannot be ignored.

———

In February 1985 the public attacks on gay men – driven by the fear of AIDS – increased. The Sun published a pronouncement by a Church of England vicar that 'homosexuals offended the Lord', and that AIDS was 'the wrath of God'. Then, on 20 February, Health Minister Kenneth Clarke announced that the government was taking unprecedented powers to detain patients in hospitals. Although he stopped short of specifying AIDS sufferers, it was clear that they were the target. Within weeks, the *Sun* published a demand, by American psychologist Paul Cameron, that 'all homosexuals should be exterminated to stop the spread of AIDS. We ought to stop pussyfooting around.'

———

JONATHAN BLAKE

HIV and AIDS became a stick to beat us with. It was all about 'gay plagues'. It was we who had brought it into the heterosexual population. You got all that sort of press coverage, which is why I didn't want to tell my parents, because of all the misinformation around.

———

As the coal strike entered its eleventh month, the government was also deploying misinformation against the miners. The weight of the Conservative Party's political machine was thrown into manipulating the media to portray the dispute as a not simply a battle with the NUM but as an existential fight between good and evil.

Across Britain – and especially in the coalfields – the government spent more than £4 million on newspaper adverts intended to have a demoralising effect on the striking miners and their families.

Alongside this 'soft-power' campaign, the government ramped up its use of the police as a *de facto* paramilitary force.

––––

SÎAN JAMES

The thing I can't forgive the government for was the police. I do not think the police today would do what the police did in 1984. I think today chief constables would refuse to be the government's private army. But in 1984 everything was set: the government had a police force – several police forces, in fact – that were co-operative and they were prepared to play that private-army role.

––––

Nor were the police the only forces ranged against the miners and their communities. MI5 would later admit that it agents were deployed to investigate anyone believed to be 'using the strike for political purposes.'

––––

HYWEL FRANCIS

My phone was definitely tapped. There were clicks on the line and, on occasion, an official in the union office picked up his phone only to hear a tape recording playing of one of his colleagues who was speaking in the next-door office: there was his voice coming down the phone.

And there were telephone engineers outside my house always – all the bloody time. I'd never seen telephone engineers there ever before. So we all realised that this was a real life-and-death struggle. The government was using any and every means to defeat the miners.

I knew that, as a historian, I should be recording this. But I was also aware that not just was it unsafe to use the phone, [but that] I shouldn't be taking notes of conversations – let alone tape recording people. And so I deliberately censored my own notebooks throughout the strike.

———

Throughout the early winter months of 1984, LGSM members continued to raise money on the streets of London for the beleaguered South Wales mining communities. But, as well as regularly providing thousands of pounds to fund the food parcels which were keeping the Neath, Dulais and Upper Swansea Valleys alive, the gay activists also responded to the growing needs of the women running the support group.

———

HYWEL FRANCIS

Within the support group there was a women's support group. It was only created after a serious political discussion about whether it was needed. The older miners – all men, of course – said that it was unnecessary and that the support group's job was only to put food in the bellies of the families and clothes on their children's backs. The women – and I supported them

– wanted to be autonomous of the men and to meet separately to do their own political action on picket lines or at meetings.

In the end, the women's group was set up and I had a discussion with Mike Jackson about the best way to support it. The answer was a mini-bus, but the women couldn't see how to get it through the overall support group; couldn't see how they would get its agreement.

CHRISTINE POWELL

That van was vitally needed for transporting the food parcels as well as other support groups who came down to see us. We had tried to borrow one from the rugby club. The club itself was fine about this but the insurance company said that, if the van was lent to our support group, the insurance would be invalid.

HYWEL FRANCIS

So Mike and I agreed that the best thing was for LGSM not to give the next tranche of money to the support group but to announce that they'd bought us a mini-bus with the funds gays and lesbians had raised. To present us with a *fait accompli*. And from the moment it arrived, it was used mostly by the women's support group.

———

But acknowledging the gift re-awakened some of the old fears and prejudices in the very traditional valley communities.

———

JAYNE FRANCIS-HEADON

We wanted to put the LGSM badge on the van. Some of the

men in the support-group committee opposed this because they said they didn't see it as necessary. But I think it was really about stigma – the stigma of having a gay logo on the van: it was too overt. But, in the end, they were won over.

HYWEL FRANCIS

I drove the van on various missions and quickly realised that the LGSM logo on the side was attracting a lot of curious glances. And I learned we had to be careful about where this could be seen. While it was OK for the LGSM logo to be seen in the parts of the constituency with mines and miners, in other more rural parts, they covered the bloody sign so people couldn't see it.

JAYNE FRANCIS-HEADON

It did cause a stir in the villages: people did a double-take when they saw the LGSM logo on the side of the van and they would say things to us. I remember stopping at the petrol station once and we were asked if all of us in the van were 'a bunch of lesbians'. And so we said yes – 'Oh yes, we are – all of us!'

SÎAN JAMES

You'd be going past someone and you'd wind the window down and he would say, 'Are you lesbians?' And we'd say, 'Yeah! Are you coming with us?' Now that person would go home and say, 'There was a van down in Treorchy today and it was all painted up with a pink triangle.'

Now, before the strike, an awful lot of people didn't know what a pink triangle was or what it stood for. They did after

LGSM: even if they didn't know or take on board the complete story, there was this awareness-raising and any fear was diffused.

CHRISTINE POWELL

That van – with 'that' logo on the side – helped changed attitudes. It wasn't just a symbol of the relationship between LGSM and our support group; it was a very, very important and practical tool for us in the valleys.

JAYNE FRANCIS-HEADON

LGSM was a significant factor in keeping us afloat with their donations. And then the van was vital in enabling us women to collect clothing and food for distribution. It opened up huge opportunities for us as a community but it also epitomised everything LGSM did for us.

———

But towards the end of February, it was becoming clear that the miner's struggle was unsustainable.

———

JAYNE FRANCIS-HEADON

People began talking about a return to work. My mum wasn't keen on that. It was funny: she hadn't wanted the men to come out on strike but then she didn't want the men to go back. But, because of everything that was happening in England and the lack of support from other unions, everybody was just caving.

It had been a long strike and a fight that they'd fought so hard, and yet it still didn't get anywhere. It was a defeat, wasn't it? That was the attitude of everybody – it was a defeat.

There was a sense of real deflation. We had made this different life for ourselves. The women had a purpose and they'd found their voices and their feet, and they'd been through all this in one year and met all these people. Now it was, 'Where do we go from here?'

———

On the last Friday in February, LGSM members travelled once again from London to the Dulais Valley.

———

BRETT HARAN

It was the weekend before they went back to work. I think we knew that this was coming: although we had a good time there, and we were welcomed just as before, there was a feeling of despondency.

CLIVE BRADLEY

It was clear that the strike was going to fail. It was obvious that it was going to be just a matter of days. And it was very emotional: everybody was very upset and angry. Some of the miners told us that they weren't going to give in – that they were going to stay on strike – but they changed their minds the next morning.

CHRISTINE POWELL

We had our meeting on the Sunday night in the Onllwyn miners' welfare hall. As you can imagine, the tone of the meeting was very subdued. I mean, I was the wife of a striking miner and this had been a huge chunk of our lives for a whole year.

With hindsight, I can see that it was always going to end badly, because Thatcher would have sunk this island before giving any concessions. So it was inevitable but, when you're on this train, so to speak, you don't think about it.

SÎAN JAMES

LGSM were with us that weekend – and that was very important. We all sat in here in my house with my parents – because they had got to know all our parents as well – and the atmosphere was dreadful. We all watched the news on TV and found that the decision had been made to go back.

RAY GOODSPEED

When it was announced, it was a bolt out of the blue. We'd known they were considering ending the strike but, when the news came through, there were miners weeping and wailing. They were furious and upset and bitter with some of the union leadership. Not with Scargill, though, because he was outvoted by the South Wales union leadership, who pushed to go back to work.

––––

Statement of Arthur Scargill: Sunday, 3 March 1985
'We face not an employer but a government, aided and abetted by the judiciary, the police and you people in the media.'

––––

RAY GOODSPEED

That's why it was particularly painful – because the motion to go back was moved by South Wales. The Dulais miners were also angry with the scabs, the police, with everybody. They were utterly crushed and defeated. It was a very bitter time and I still find it difficult to talk about it.

SÎAN JAMES

I remember sitting there and shouting at the television and my mother saying to me, 'You don't want this strike to end, do you?' Inside, I didn't want it to end because I was afraid that, if the strike ended, life would go back to what it was before – a very traditional life – and that all the friends we'd made would disappear.

———

On Monday, 4 March 1985, led by colliery bands and union banners, the striking miners marched back to resume work at their pits.

———

RAY GOODSPEED

I watched the march back to work on TV. It was horrible. I was in floods of tears. I was sobbing. It tore my guts out. The dignity of the march back made it worse, somehow.

BRETT HARAN

When the men actually went back, it felt like a kick in the stomach; it was a massive blow and the Tories were so utterly triumphalist.

———

Some of the families of striking miners had already had a foretaste of what victory for the government and the forces of business would mean.

JAYNE FRANCIS-HEADON

On the day the men went back, I was working in a local shirt factory. Many of the miners' wives had worked there and, throughout the strike, they had worked long hours there to keep families going. But the managers had kept putting the targets up, just to take advantage of these desperate women. The women couldn't hit these targets so they didn't get their full bonuses, and the managers used to revel in the fact that they were doing this, upping the targets. So many of the women were glad, in one way, that their men were going back to work.

―――

But for others, the end of the strike – and the lessons learned in a year of hardship – also held out the promise of a new life based on respect and understanding.

―――

BRETT HARAN

Once I'd got over the feeling of despondency, I realised that we had got some momentum as a result of LGSM; there was something coming out of the strike which we could take forward. Even though that strike was a defeat, we had brought two communities together who, on the face of it, had nothing in common. Two communities of which, before the strike, people would have said, 'Why should they make common cause? Surely that's doomed?'

SÎAN JAMES

I used to say that the strike was like a fast track to find out anything you wanted to find out about, politically. We met people who were Maoists, others who were Euro-communists, and one person used to preface every sentence with the phrase 'the running dogs of capitalism'.

DAI DONOVAN

I absolutely believe that the arrival of LGSM in our valleys changed those communities. It's not often you meet twenty-five people in one room and you like every single one. They were generous, kind-hearted, articulate, intelligent: how could I not like them? You would have to have a heart of stone to ignore all that and say, 'I don't like you because you're gay.'

BRETT HARAN

Our whole experience in Dulais reassured me that, actually, you can make those alliances and connections between people whose lives appear, superficially, to be very different. You can make people see that, despite those differences, we have far more in common than that which divides us.

DAI DONOVAN

We knew, under Thatcher, that all trades unionists would be under attack and, with LGSM, I met people who had genuinely been suffering harassment and yet they had shown such generosity to us – and we had to repay it.

CHAPTER FOURTEEN

UNITY

The miners had lost. Mrs Thatcher and the Conservative Party had triumphed, gaining revenge on the NUM for its defeats of the Heath government in 1972 and 1974. Very quickly the National Coal Board began closing 'uneconomic pits' across Britain's coalfields. In the valleys of South Wales, nine collieries would be shuttered in 1985 alone.

———

HYWEL FRANCIS

We had sustained our miners and their families during the year of the strike but, after it, many of them had a terrible time. They lost their jobs, their families fell apart and they fell deeply into debt.

JAYNE FRANCIS-HEADON

I started to realise that there wasn't anything for me if I stayed in Wales. I had the thought that I should join the army. Well, that disgusted my mother. She saw the army as Maggie's boot boys but I thought of it differently: I didn't see it as me working for Maggie Thatcher – I saw it as her having to give me money. And so I left the valleys and joined the army.

––––

For some, the bitterness of defeat was tempered by a pride in the courage shown by the mining communities throughout the year-long strike.

––––

DAI DONOVAN

Although we did lose, it was a success because we didn't sit on our knees – we fought. Many thousands of people can look themselves in the eye and know that they fought. To me, it's not the bloody losing; it's about *how* you lost. And I think we grow from that.

––––

But, for others, that spring of 1985 was a time for the unions and the political left to learn the hard lessons of defeat.

––––

HYWEL FRANCIS

We lost because we did not have unity among the miners themselves. We also did not have unity between the miners and the rest of the trade-union movement. And we didn't have unity between the trade-union movement and wider British society. Some of us had tried to make the strike a broader political struggle but, sadly, that wasn't the thrust of the main NUM struggle. The NUM leadership confused mass pickets with a mass movement. We thought we had the latter but all we had was mass pickets.

In the end, the strike lacked any real understanding of the great forces massed against us. It wasn't just the government; it was the whole of the British State which was thrown at us – a national police force, as well as the British army.

———

Yet, within pain and suffering of the miners' strike, there were also rays of hope and these pointed the way to building new – and much needed – alliances.

———

DAI DONOVAN

I don't know the answer to this but I pose the question: did the introduction of the strike into lesbian and gay communities stop them arguing and bring them together under a broader banner? That the home they should have been looking to was there already: the working-class trade-union movement?

BRETT HARAN

Mrs Thatcher was in the ascendancy and we knew that we would soon have to gear up for another fight. Certainly, anti-gay stuff was coming and there was also a feeling that the Labour Party – and Neil Kinnock – should be doing more.

DAI DONOVAN

I think the strike helped them see that their cause needed to be fought out against that background, in that forum and with those allies; that the important thing wasn't your issues as a lesbian or your issues as a gay man, but that there were other important things and we all need to see ourselves as part of that wider movement.

BRETT HARAN

At the time of the strike, gay rights just hadn't made a break-through into the national Labour Party.

They were seen by the Party hierarchy as a peripheral thing; maybe something that was an embarrassment, and certainly not a relevant or pressing political issue. And, at the same time, the Tories were pushing an agenda – especially in London – that Labour was beset by the 'Loony Left'; that these people could never be trusted. And if there was any notion that Labour was associated with lesbian and gay rights, the Tories were going to hammer them. And that's why Kinnock and the Labour Party leadership tried to distance themselves from the issue. They felt it was a massive stick to beat the Labour Party with. They were just too nervous, too wary, too cautious. There were terrified.

———

Although some of its members were actively trying to change the Labour Party's opposition to gay rights, as a group, LGSM decided to reach out directly to the union movement, despite its chequered history on the issue.

———

PAUL CANNING

Homophobia ran all the way through unions. There was no

anti-discrimination law at all at that time, and the unions weren't defending gay people. People could be fired – especially teachers – for being gay and there was no history of unions defending them.

———

And the union LGSM chose – the National Union of Mineworkers – had never officially supported the struggle of lesbian and gay men for equal rights.

———

RAY GOODSPEED

Before the strike, I felt that Arthur Scargill was just dismissive of gay rights. He'd previously been buttonholed by gay campaigners outside the Labour Party conference, who were trying to get homosexual equality motions through conference for years to no effect. Scargill just brushed them to one side. He was dismissive and his attitude, effectively, was, 'Don't be ridiculous. I'm from the NUM.'

He came from an old-style Stalinist hardline background: I felt he had no time for any of this stuff because 'It wasn't about the workers, was it?' To my mind, his attitude was, 'I'm a miner – miners aren't gay. They're solid, masculine, working-class people. Gay miners couldn't exist because gay people are all interior decorators and ballet dancers.' That sort of attitude.

———

But the alliance formed between the young gay activists and the mining families of the Neath, Dulais and Upper Swansea Valleys convinced LGSM that at least some in the union could be persuaded to change their stance.

MIKE JACKSON

One of the wonderful things the miners did early on was to wear our badges. We hadn't asked for that – they just did it. They worked out that wearing our badge was the best thing that they could do for us. And they went on picket lines all over Britain – facing up to big, burly coppers and other big, burly miners – wearing a gay badge.

And so, three months after the strike ended, we asked the miners to march with us at Gay Pride.

CLIVE BRADLEY

In 1985 Pride was much smaller than it is now: probably no more than 10,000 people altogether. It was political with quite a large 'P'. It was then understood as a political event, rather than the carnival it has now become.

_____

But as June approached and the date of the march came ever closer, there was no certainty that the miners would turn up.

_____

MIKE JACKSON

We'd publicised in *Capital Gay* that the miners would be coming but I don't think people believed that they would.

DAVE LEWIS

I had a bit of anxiety because some people could argue that the relationship had been one-way. They needed our support and we gave it to them. I hoped that it would come the other way but we didn't actually know whether it would. You know:

they could just have said, 'Oh, yeah, yeah, yeah,' and then not turn up.

PAUL CANNING

At that point, there wasn't any real history of the trades unions being at Pride. We'd never even seen straight people on the Gay Pride march.

This would have been really the first time that there had been any serious trades-union presence; the first time that a major trades-union had come along.

———

As they assembled at the starting point in Hyde Park, LGSM's activists had decided that – whether or not the miners arrived – they would march in the middle of the parade.

———

MIKE JACKSON

We had discussed in a meeting whether we should ask to lead the parade – some people were saying that we were the best thing since sliced bread; that nothing like us had happened in the lesbian and gay movement for years and years and years. But, in the end, we'd decided not to and that we would walk with the Labour and trade-union movement. But then the miners arrived, carrying this huge silk lodge banner from Blaenant.

MARTIN GOODSELL

I felt a real sense of achievement when the miners turned up. I'd been involved in the Labour Campaign for Gay Rights and that meant working in a particular way – passing motions and going to trades-union branches. But at that Pride, I had an overwhelming sense of having built something that was solid and lasting.

MIKE JACKSON

People were coming into the park and saying in disbelief, 'Oh my God, the miners *are* here.'

The miners and families from Dulais had arrived in the red mini-bus LGSM had donated and a large coach that was full of people, some of whom we hadn't met before; people from other villages along the valley.

PAUL CANNING

That was just a really big hit. This was the NUM. Nor was it just the Dulais people: there were others from different regions.

MIKE JACKSON

And as they were assembling the lodge banner – it's such a big piece of kit – the crowd just gathered around us and then wouldn't move until, eventually, someone from the Pride committee said, 'You'll have to lead the march – there's just too many of you and we'll never get you out if you don't.'

So, by default, we did lead the march that year and I remember this bank of photographers with flashbulbs going off and thinking, 'Wow, this is good…' At the very front was the Pride '85 banner, then LGSM's and, behind it – between it and the huge Blaenant banner right at the back of our contingent – were easily a thousand people. It was incredible, that presence.

WENDY CALDON

It was fantastically important that the miners came to support us and it was absolutely right that they were there. I would have been amazed if they hadn't come because I think they enjoyed themselves when they came to see us.

We had had discos and dancing and bonkers meals. We were friends and comrades and allies.

MIKE JACKSON

But although the South Wales miners turned up, the national union didn't. The NUM had got a message of support to LGSM in our first few weeks of existence: Heathfield, McGahey and Scargill sent a message saying, 'NUM supports lesbian and gay rights. Your struggle is our struggle.' So, officially, they'd acknowledged us early on. But the strike was enormous and, when you think about it, there were just ten or fifteen of us at the inner core of LGSM, supporting a tiny community in a remote part of South Wales, so is it something the national union would – in June 1985 – have thought it was important to support? Don't forget: this is three months after the strike, after everybody's been beaten. And, in the end, we were happy enough to have the Welsh contingent because they were our brothers and sisters – our friends, by this stage.

WENDY CALDON

We took our LAPC banner to Pride '85 and we were singing our song 'every woman is a lesbian at heart'. That is what we always sang – 'every woman is a lesbian at heart/this is what we find'.

BRETT HARAN

There was a very heavy police presence: they were lining the streets as if we were these marauding hordes who were about to bring down the apparatus of the State. The coppers were looking at us as if we were, indeed, 'the enemy within'. Don't forget: the prevailing attitude to gay people was still very hostile. The Tories were in full pomp and were demonising us; the police were triumphant in the aftermath of the strike. It was still very much 'us and them'.

WENDY CALDON

We used to get a few fascists who'd stand there and shout, 'You f-ing homos.' So it was one of the best moments of my life when Sîan James stood up on the Pride march and made an amazing speech.

She said, 'If my child comes to me and tells me they are gay, I will understand.' That was huge in 1985 – a huge thing for someone to say. I was really moved by that. Later on in the day, we ran to each other and hugged, and I remember her saying, 'I'm hugging a lesbian and I'm absolutely fine about it.' I have never forgotten that and I shall never forget that: it was life changing.

MIKE JACKSON

The arrival of the South Wales mining contingent on that march meant everything to me. Immense pride.

We had had our detractors within the lesbian and gay movement: there had been a storm of letters in *Capital Gay*, typically asking, 'What have the miners ever done for us?' Which was a valid thing to say. Yet here we were, fifteen months later and here's the miners on the Pride march.

BRETT HARAN

For me, there was a massive sense of validation and acceptance. Dai Donovan had said, 'You've worn our badge and, when the time comes, we'll wear yours with pride.' The fact was that we had made those bonds and those connections and they didn't just fizzle out when the strike ended. There was something tangible – and it survived.

MARTIN GOODSELL

And I knew then we had something we could build on; I knew that we were going places and that this was the start of something even bigger.

The miners' historic support at the 1985 Pride march was a bridgehead into the wider union movement. Throughout the summer, LGSM's activists built on it to pressure the Labour Party into putting gay rights on the agenda for that year's conference.

COLIN CLEWS

There had been previous attempts to get gay rights adopted by the Labour Party but there wasn't the groundswell of support to make it happen. In the early 1980s, gay activists had tried to get the issue of homosexual rights taken up by our unions. We formed units within our unions to lobby but these units weren't big enough to break through.

MARTIN GOODSELL
The Labour Party leadership was socially conservative and cautious. Lots of people had been doing work to change this: there were a lot of lesbian and gay trades-union groups, which had been doing a lot of work within them and within the Labour party.

RAY GOODSPEED
Motions had been put up to conference before and voted down, but there was a view on the left, in general, that to be gay was to be middle class. There was this view that it was something middle-class gays did – that they corrupted working-class boys.

CLIVE BRADLEY
The notion that homosexuality was a middle-class affectation imposed on the working class goes back to the nineteenth century and the Oscar Wilde type of aristocrat, who would pay to have sex with telegraph boys or guardsmen.

RAY GOODSPEED
The Labour Party, historically, didn't see gay rights as something to focus on. It was regarded as a bit of a personal issue, a bit of a tragedy, a bit of a sickness, a bit dangerous and a bit pathetic. It wasn't a case of, 'I'm a socialist, therefore I must support gay rights.'

It wasn't seen as an issue of justice and equality. And gays were presumed to be middle-class histrionic types living in central London. They certainly weren't presumed to work in the steelworks or down the mines.

———

By the date of the conference in October, the activists had enough grass-roots support to ensure that a motion committing Labour to backing gay rights would be put to a vote.

———

PAUL CANNING
But there was absolutely no guarantee it would pass, because the leadership was strongly opposed to it and there were hardly any MPs who backed it.

MARTIN GOODSELL
When that motion went to the conference, the powers that be tried to get it remitted; to get it removed from the agenda. The main concern was around the age of consent – that was the hot potato; that was what the Labour leadership and the unions were worried about.

COLIN CLEWS
But what had happened with LGSM changed everything. The NUM came on board with us. And we didn't just get its support: the NUM brought with it other unions and we found, at last, that we'd got the numbers we needed.

PAUL CANNING

Ultimately, it was about taking sides. The leadership hadn't wanted to touch this issue with a barge pole. The leadership took one side but then the unions took the other. And if well-respected unions like the miners – and they *were* well respected throughout the Labour movement back then – back you, others fall in line. And that's what happened.

MARTIN GOODSELL

In the end, we won by 600,000 votes – and that was the trade-union blocks pushing it through. But what mattered was the motion was passed. It was the first time a gay-rights motion got through a Labour Party conference.

SÎAN JAMES

I was doing fringe meetings and conferences with LGSM at the conference. We were pushing for recognition and protection for gay men and lesbian women. So many of the friends we had met had told us stories about having no rights, of being kicked out of their houses when their partners died after long-term relationships. They could not inherit property or the right to pensions. They could be sacked for being gay and they couldn't win a tribunal for unfair dismissal on those grounds that you were gay. We talked about how we needed to correct this and we needed to give people their rights; how giving gay men and women equality under the law is not a gift – it's a right. And I do not believe that we would have achieved what we did if it hadn't been for us getting involved with LGSM.

NICOLA FIELD

LGSM was a little trigger: it had a catalyst effect, but the policy of the NUM did not change just because of LGSM. There were gay-rights motions coming down from Yorkshire – the crucible of the strike. As well, anti-inequality policies started to filter through from all over.

PAUL CANNING

The thing that absolutely swung it was the miners and the fact that they were supporting us. I think you can say the NUM backing us was the tipping point. And that wouldn't have happened without LGSM: absolutely no way it would have happened.

WENDY CALDON

It wouldn't have happened without LGSM. To have a big macho union like the miners saying 'we support gay rights': that was a watershed moment.

GETHIN ROBERTS

The attitude to gays and lesbians changed among the grass-roots union members relatively quickly. I don't think it changed so fast in the leadership of the unions. I spoke to Scargill after the NUM leadership had supported the resolution at the Labour Party conference. I was then working as general manager of the LSE students union and Scargill had just been elected as our honorary president.

There's a photo of me and a few others holding a big banner, welcoming him: it read 'Faggots and Dykes say "Right On, Arthur"'. I also had a print of this on my office wall and I asked Scargill to sign it; he did – but we formed the impression that he was quite uncomfortable about the whole thing.

RAY GOODSPEED

Scargill had not been focused on gay rights – but his attitude changed. It had to really, once what we'd done became known, because there were miners all over the country wearing our badges.

CLIVE BRADLEY

Whether or not Scargill personally supported us, I think he – and the union leadership – had learned a lesson. And one of the two main political parties now was committed– at least in principle – to gay rights, and that made it part of the national conversation in a very different way to previously.

PAUL CANNING

It was inevitable that the Labour Party was going to change. But having the alternative party of government was a really important thing for gay people. It would have happened anyway but LGSM and the involvement with the miners speeded things up. It wouldn't have happened for another five years, I think, otherwise.

———

But many of the activists – as well as their supporters in the unions – realised that passing a motion at the Labour conference was only a first step.

BRETT HARAN

It was tremendously uplifting. These were difficult times and gay rights were not a popular thing to be associated with. So for one of the two main political parties to commit to this was a big step forward. But, while a lot of people were won round to the idea of gay rights as a valid political issue, there was still, for many people, a sticking point around the age of consent. There was still this residual notion that an equal age of consent wasn't quite right; that, for some people, homosexuality might be just a phase and that they had to be protected. There was still further convincing to be done throughout the Labour movement.

DAVE LEWIS

The age of consent was still a major issue for many people and I knew equality in that wouldn't come for many, many years. So I saw that conference as the first step on a rather long road.

———

That road would prove to be longer even than the LGSM activists suspected. AIDS cases were growing and, with them, public hostility to gay men. Just before the historic Labour conference, city magistrates in Manchester had ordered the forcible detention of a man suspected of carrying the virus. And Mrs Thatcher would soon launch a new front in the government's war on gay rights.

CHAPTER FIFTEEN

PAY BACK

Mrs Thatcher's victory over the miners strengthened her grip on power and led, from the start of 1986, to a new and unprecedented attack on the gay community.

———

CLIVE BRADLEY

The whole Labour movement was hammered and it's hard to overstate how big a part the defeat of the miners played in that. Part of our argument for LGSM and what we did was that, if the miners lost, we – lesbians and gay men – would be screwed. And certainly the Tories tried.

NICOLA FIELD

But there were political lessons that came out of the strike, which we needed to learn. Those were lessons about how we can be defeated by our own side. Because Thatcher went for the kill after the strike.

———

Public opinion was poisoned by regular and vicious anti-gay features in the tabloid press. A column in the *Daily Star* that year, written by its deputy editor, Ray Mills, was typical:

> Little queers or big queens, Mills has had enough of them all – the lesbians, bisexuals and transsexuals, the hermaphrodites and the catamites and the gender benders who brazenly flaunt their sexual failings to the disgust and grave offence of the silent majority. A blight on them all, says Mills.

By then, at least one hundred and ten gay men had died from AIDS and Donald Acheson, Britain's Chief Medical Officer, had warned the government that 'There is no effective treatment for the infection [and] a vaccine is unlikely to be developed in the foreseeable future.'

But Mrs Thatcher and other Conservative politicians opposed any spending on health advice. The country's only HIV/AIDS-specific organisation – the Terrence Higgins Trust – had been established in 1983 but, for the first two years of its life, it was entirely dependent on charitable donations. When the GLC stepped in with £17,000 of urgently needed support, the Conservative-led Westminster Council went to court to block the grant.

And although the Labour Party was – in theory – committed

to homosexual equality, and included a gay-rights pledge in its election manifestos, Mrs Thatcher's government turned this into a political weapon.

————

COLIN CLEWS

The Conservatives felt that it was an issue with which to discredit Labour. At both a national and a local level, they were happy to buy into – and actively feed – homophobia. During the May 1986 local elections, for example, Conservatives in the London Borough of Haringey produced a leaflet declaring, 'You do not want your child to be educated by a homosexual or lesbian.'

————

That this was a conscious and deliberate attack on gay men and lesbian women was borne out in December 1986, when a Manchester chief constable addressed a national conference on how police should interact with people with AIDS.

'Everywhere I go I see evidence of people swirling around in the cesspool of their own making. Why do homosexuals freely engage in sodomy and other obnoxious sexual practices knowing the dangers involved?'

In an editorial, the *Sun* praised Anderton's stance: 'Their defiling act of love is not only unnatural, in today's world it is lethal … What Britain needs is more men like Anderton – and fewer gay terrorists holding the decent members of society to ransom.'

Mrs Thatcher, too, approved: she blocked calls for a public enquiry into Anderton's comments. Within months, she would launch an assault of her own. In the 1987 election, the

Conservatives took out billboard advertising which deployed homophobia to attack the Labour Party. One poster showed a line of young men wearing badges bearing the mottos 'Gay Pride' and 'Gay Sports Day' – together with a slogan which read, 'This is Labour's camp. Do you want to live in it?'

When the Conservatives won the 1987 general election, the government introduced a new law – Section 28 of the Local Government Act – which made it illegal for councils to 'intentionally promote homosexuality or publish material with the intention of promoting homosexuality.' Mrs Thatcher followed this up with an incendiary speech to the party conference in October: 'Children who need to be taught to respect traditional moral values are being taught that they have an inalienable right to be gay … All of those children are being cheated of a sound start in life – yes, cheated.'

––––

BRETT HARAN

I knew all this anti-gay stuff was coming. But, when I heard the Prime Minister of our country say something so stark and unequivocal – that people didn't have a right to be gay – I was shocked. I realised that we were seen by her as people who had no worth whatsoever. As if we were less than human.

––––

In December 1987 the offices of *Capital Gay* were firebombed. In Parliament, Conservative MP Elaine Kellett-Bowman unashamedly welcomed the news: 'Quite right! … I am quite prepared to affirm that there should be an intolerance of evil!'

But instead of reprimanding the MP, three months later,

Margaret Thatcher rewarded Kellet-Bowman by making her a dame – the female equivalent of a knighthood.

Mrs Thatcher also attempted to block her own government's plans for explicit public-health warnings about AIDS. She fought repeatedly to suppress a high-profile television campaign bearing the slogan 'Don't Die of Ignorance', despite figures showing that Britain had at least 610 known sufferers. By then, 293 men had died from the disease. One was LGSM's founder, Mark Ashton. But, for as long as it appeared to affect gay men, there was little public sympathy for the victims.

———

JONATHAN BLAKE

At that point, HIV and AIDS were only attacking homosexuals and they were deemed expendable. I mean, who cared about us? That was the attitude: who cares?

The only reason that changed was because of the health minister Norman Fowler, who is the one person, among all the Tories, that I do have any time for. He told Margaret Thatcher that it was in the heterosexual community and she freaked. What he didn't tell her was that this was the intravenous heterosexual drug-using community of Edinburgh. Because if she'd have known that, she'd have said, 'Let 'em die.' But because HIV and AIDS were now seen to be in the heterosexual community, the State poured millions into them.

RAY GOODSPEED

The whole problem was that it hadn't really been spoken about. After the huge HIV/AIDS publicity campaign, it *had* to be talked about, because it was on television. And because of that, you had gay people – ordinary gay people who didn't look like men in rain macs, or sordid, sad pathetic creatures – talking about being homosexual on TV. And that changed the climate.

MIKE JACKSON

I think one of the most damaging things about the oppression of the lesbian and gay community, historically, is that we weren't even listened to. We were just ignored. So you couldn't have an argument or a debate: we were just silenced.

——

In February 1994, Parliament, with the support of Conservative Prime Minister John Major, voted to lower the age of consent for male homosexual acts from twenty-one to eighteen. Although this only reduced – rather than abolished – the discrimination, leaving the age of consent for gay men higher than for heterosexuals, it marked a first shift away from the aggressively anti-gay stance of his predecessor, Margaret Thatcher.

But it was not until 1997 – and the election of a Labour government – that the commitment to equal rights fought for by LGSM and its fellow activists began to be realised.

——

MIKE JACKSON

We're all terribly aware that there's a great danger of LGSM being over-egged, as if we were responsible for everything, which would be a travesty because there were people beavering away in the Labour and trades-union movements decades before us. Really, we were a part of a continuum of activists, but I do think we helped accelerate that gradual process of change.

————

The first victory was the abolition on the ban on lesbians and gay men serving in the armed forces.

————

JAYNE FRANCIS-HEADON

Before the year 2000, the military didn't allow any gay or lesbian anything. If they found you, you were out – that was it. And we had lectures – warning about being approached by other women. Like a scaremongering thing, it was; making us all scared about the chance of dishonourable discharge. And a lot of girls in my platoon were very worried about the higher ranks of women who might make advances to them. They were in that naïve place that I was in when I was sixteen and before I met LGSM.

I wasn't gay at that point – but I wasn't against being gay either. And I know that, if I hadn't gone through the strike and met LGSM, I would have been very frightened, like the other girls in my platoon.

————

In the years that followed, there would be a succession of victories for gay rights. In 2001 the homosexual age of consent was lowered to sixteen – the same as for heterosexual couples. Two years later, Section 28 was repealed, without a single prosecution ever having taken place. Civil partnerships were introduced in 2005 and, in March 2014, the first gay weddings were held after Parliament passed the Same-Sex Marriage Act.

The era of state-sponsored persecution on the grounds of sexuality was over, and a promise made more than a quarter of a century earlier had been kept.

———

DAI DONOVAN

While we felt the uniqueness of our relationship at the time – we in seeking the gay community's assistance, and they in becoming involved publicly in this major strike – I don't think any of us realised that, thirty years later, those events could have led to gay marriage and an acceptance by all that it was an individual's right to live their life as a gay person openly and without fear of censure or attack.

What I do know is that, with LGSM, I met people who had genuinely been suffering. These were people who had been identified as a group simply because of a characteristic that the establishment despised. And instead of saying to us, 'You miners, whingeing about the police: get used to it because we've had to,' they were so generous that they wanted to help us. And, in the end, we repaid it.

CHAPTER SIXTEEN

CHANGE

In April 2015 two MPs left their offices in Parliament for the last time. Both had represented their constituencies for many years, before deciding not to stand again at the 2015 general election. Hywel Francis and Sîan James had been pivotal figures in the miners' strike, and the alliance between the South Wales coalfield and LGSM had changed the course of their personal – as well as political – lives.

———

SÎAN JAMES

I'd married at sixteen. At twenty, I had two children and was happy as a housewife and young mother. As long as my lace curtains were the cleanest, my children immaculately dressed, their hand-knitted clothes made with love, I was happy. I – and all my friends – came from very loving families and we knew what we wanted out of life. Then along came the strike. For a whole year.

And when it finished, I remember one very big, important trade unionist saying to me, 'Now that the strike is over, you'd better get back to the kitchen where you belong.' But, after meeting the people I had met during the strike, I realised that the difference between all the people who were telling us what we should be doing and all of us who were doing the doing was that they had a degree and I didn't.

So if saw I wanted to be one of the people making the decisions, or influencing decisions, I'd have to get myself a further education, and that meant getting a degree. That was the big light-bulb moment for me. And so many of LGSM were so supportive: they encouraged me and told me that my opinion was just as valid as anybody else's.

——

Sîan went to Swansea University, graduated with a degree in Welsh and, in 2005, was elected as a Labour MP – the first woman to represent Swansea East in the House of Commons. Five years earlier, her compatriot from the support group, Hywel Francis, had been elected as Labour MP for Aberavon, the constituency at the bottom end of the Dulais Valley: he, too, had come to understand the legacy of LGSM's involvement with his communities.

——

HYWEL FRANCIS

During the strike, there were all kinds of relationships built up with all kinds of groups and people. The only one which has stood the test of time is the relationship with the gays and lesbians. It has been sustained over the years. And those relationship actually grew out of the end of the strike.

CHRISTINE POWELL

Because of LGSM, the communities began to change – slowly and gradually. Previously, the attitude had been that these people – gays – existed, but not in our world.

DAI DONOVAN

I absolutely believe that the arrival of LGSM in our valleys changed those communities. When you were living there in that time, it didn't necessarily seem like they were closed communities but certainly you can say that the conversations wouldn't have been about health issues for gay people.

MIKE JACKSON

To have that dialogue – that deep, personal conversation – with the community in Dulais melted away all the demonisation. We could speak to one another and they realised that gay people didn't eat babies for breakfast; we were just like them really. It was an opportunity to say to those people, 'We're just like you. We just sleep with people of the same sex – that's our only difference.'

CHRISTINE POWELL

Like a lot of phobias, the community's fear was born of ignorance: if you'd never actually met a gay person, how could you know that they didn't have two heads? Once the community met them, people saw that gays didn't have two heads or four arms – and that it was safe to shake hands with them.

DAI DONOVAN

And, by the end of the strike, when AIDS became a big issue, there were people in our villages talking about that. And not talking about it from the perspective of fear, but from the perspective of genuine empathy and compassion.

———

One man came to symbolise the impact of LGSM in the South Wales coalfields. Cliff Grist was a former miner and had been a mainstay of the support group during the strike. But, for years, he had hidden his sexuality from his community.

———

SÎAN JAMES

People didn't really know that Cliff was gay. Because he never had a girlfriend, people would have thought, 'Oh, he's just devoted to his mother,' or, 'He's a mummy's boy.' I think Cliff's whole experience was of being in a community where being part of a couple was the norm. And he once confided in me that he'd lived a very lonely life: he obviously must have had partners but, for many years, he'd lived a very solitary existence.

BRETT HARAN

Just imagine: he was in his mid-fifties and he'd lived in the valleys all his life. He'd had some sort of gay life but a very closeted one. He certainly hadn't felt able to come out. And then, suddenly, these twenty-seven gay guys arrive from London. He was in his element. His eyes lit up when we got there.

SÎAN JAMES

He said that his life changed drastically when LGSM came to visit. I took that to mean that, for the first time, he saw that there was an alternative way to live a good, fulfilling life as a gay man. Once they'd been down here, you could see the difference in him. He was mixing with very articulate young men who were living the sort of lives he hadn't been able to.

HYWEL FRANCIS

He used to look forward to LGSM's visits for weeks in advance. I would meet him in the street and he'd say, 'The gays are coming down this weekend.' It was such a big thing for him. And so he symbolises something, doesn't he? In many ways, he personified the relationship between this valley and LGSM.

———

Nor was Cliff Grist an isolated example.

———

STEPHANIE CHAMBERS

There were lesbian women in the Dulais Valley who knew they were lesbians, but who weren't out. We brought sexual politics on to their agenda. We gave them no choice. There were men dancing together in Onllwyn miner's welfare. I danced with both men and women there – and I remember snogging some of the women. In fact, it was more than a snog. So I think we contributed to a gradual process of change in attitudes within the South Wales mining valleys.

———

In the years that followed the end of the strike, LGSM's influence – and friendship – made it less difficult for gay men and women to live openly in those communities.

———

JAYNE FRANCIS-HEADON

The impact of LGSM was to instil a friendship between people who would otherwise probably never have met, and it opened up acceptance of diversity.

Today a gay man or a lesbian woman in the valleys would not be shunned or alienated: they may not always have the easiest time, because things there remain stereotypically 'small Welsh village', but their sexuality would be accepted now.

BRET HARAN

If we left one small mark in those communities, it was the realisation and acceptance that gay people were not perverts, we were not 'other'; we were their brothers and sisters, their sons and daughters, and sometimes their mothers and fathers. And, if contact with us made it easier for a gay man or a lesbian to come out in those communities and have a much happier experience, that is an amazing thing. And I know it did.

SÎAN JAMES

We take gay rights in our stride today. My fourteen-year-old granddaughter talks about girls in her school who have girlfriends; there is a young man in the rugby team who has come out as gay. They can't see how it was back then in the early and mid-1980s.

NICOLA FIELD

I know it became easier for young people in those South Wales communities to come out as gay. When we went to Dulais in 2015, I met LGBT people in their thirties who had grown up in those valleys and who said they had no problem because the community was, by then, gay-friendly. It was amazing to meet these ebullient, self-loving people, who had grown up and been allowed to be themselves.

RAY GOODSPEED

We've heard stories in the years since of miner's sons who have felt able to come out and his dad was fine with his homosexuality because he remembered the strike. We haven't cured the world of homophobia but we did change attitudes in the valleys. Certainly in Onllwyn, a couple of the children of those we stayed with have since come out as gay – including Hefina's daughter.

JAYNE FRANCIS-HEADON

I'm a lesbian now, and married to a woman, and maybe that was inside me all that time. I never sat down and really thought about it. But I ask myself, 'Did that time in 1984 and 1985 with LGSM give me the chance to one day be who I wanted to be?' I don't know for sure – but I think it did.

HYWEL FRANCIS

The involvement with LGSM made it immeasurably easier for gay men and women to grow up and live in these valleys.

We now have a local gay icon: Bethan Kelland-Howell is a lesbian, captain of Seven Sisters rugby club – and the daughter of one of our striking miners.

CHRISTINE POWELL

Last year the club hosted her gay marriage. Now this is a club which was once pretty much made up of striking miners. Can you imagine that happening before the strike and LGSM came here?

MIKE JACKSON

When we went down to Onllwyn in 2015, we met that lesbian, very-out rugby player who had just got married to her partner at Crynant rugby ground. Three hundred people had come out to support her on that day. She was completely out in her community – and everybody loved her and her partner. That's how much things have changed.

CLIVE BRADLEY

But it's also important to realise that the transformative power of LGSM wasn't just in one direction. It wasn't just a case of these worthy cosmopolitan Londoners bringing pasta and opera to the remote valleys of Wales. I think there's a very great danger of imaging that the miners were politically ignorant and needed us to enlighten them. These were communities that had generations of miners who had a radical tradition – they'd been involved in the General Strike – and they didn't need lefties from London to tell them about all this stuff.

STEPHANIE CHAMBERS

It had a massive influence on me. It opened my eyes and made me understand how Thatcher was stripping this country. Before going to Dulais, I didn't have a clue; didn't know how it was all working. But when I did, I got very angry. When I went there, I saw how communities come together to get through. And I was so proud to be a part of that.

CLIVE BRADLEY

The reason I'm still a socialist, thirty-two years on, is partly because I saw and experienced their struggle. Even though those communities were ultimately defeated, that experience gave me something which affected the rest of my life. People who haven't witnessed that – have never experienced anything like that – find it easy to say, 'Oh, that's the way the world is and nothing is ever going to change.' When you've witnessed a huge struggle like that, and played a small part in it, it has a transformative effect on you.

MIKE JACKSON

They taught me the meaning of the word 'comradeship'. I'd worked previously with lesbian and gay activists and, of course, there was a sense of common cause with them. But that was nothing compared to the comradeship I got from working within the traditional strong communities in South Wales. We learned such a lot from them.

CHAPTER SEVENTEEN

PRIDE

For more than twenty years after the end of the miners' strike, the story of LGSM, and of the common cause found by its young gay activists with the struggling valleys of the South Wales coalfield, gradually faded from view.

———

SÎAN JAMES

Within our community, the story of LGSM was known: if you grew up there, you knew it. But what we didn't realise was that what we had done was so out of the ordinary.

JAYNE FRANCIS-HEADON

I told the story many times over the years, to as many people as would listen. But people didn't believe it. They couldn't believe that in the 1980s people were in such poverty and that we didn't have food and that we were supported by lesbians and gays.

———

Even within the gay community, LGSM's actions had become a kind of folk-myth – something woven deep into the fabric of memory but largely forgotten or disbelieved. Stephen Beresford – the writer who created and would finally script *Pride*, the movie – first heard the story in the early 1990s.

> I was in a relationship, with someone who was ten years older than me, and we were having a row. He was talking about how gay men of my generation weren't political … And he started to tell me as much as he knew – which was not much – of the legend of LGSM. And this incredible story of mutual support – unexpected mutual support – came up. And I remember thinking … I don't believe it's true … but if this story is true I'm going to find it out and I'm going to write it up…[12]

In those pre-Google days, it was difficult to track down LGSM's members. Even when he did, it would be more than a decade before Stephen Beresford found a backer willing to fund his script about 'vegan lesbian activists and a coal mining dispute.'

———

STEPHANIE CHAMBERS.

When I heard they were making a film, I couldn't believe it. I thought, 'Who's going to come and watch a film about lesbians and gay men supporting the miners thirty years ago?' We'd been invisible for so long.

---

[12] Stephen Beresford interviewed on stage at the British Film Institute, 2015.

STEPHEN BERESFORD

I often describe it as a lost story, and many of the people – the real people involved – said to me, 'We all thought this story would die with us, so bring it to the world and, you know, their achievement to the world is a marvellous feeling.[13]

———

Pride opened in British cinemas in September 2014. Within six months, it had garnered a succession of international prizes and nominations, including the prestigious Golden Globe and British Academy Film Awards.

———

JAYNE FRANCIS-HEADON

When the film came out, there was a special screening in London and my partner, Emily, came with me. She cried all the way through it and, on the way home, she said to me, 'I can't believe that story you told was true.' And I knew what she meant: it *is* a story that people find hard to believe – they didn't think I was lying, but the extent of what happened, well – it is hard to believe. And I'm proud of our story. And of what we all did.[14]

STEPHANIE CHAMBERS

The film made us visible worldwide. And that had a very profound personal effect. I finally came out at work: I had to because I was going up to London for a red-carpet première. And when I came out, I found that I got applause.

---

[13] Stephen Beresford: winners press-conference interview, BAFTA, 2015.
[14] Sadly, Jayne's mother – the redoubtable Hefina Headon – died before the film was completed.

NICOLA FIELD

I was initially suspicious of this mainstream film about us. There were a lot of wounds from the experience of that time for me. And these were re-opened when the film came out. There was the experience of feeling that I had been the only female in LGSM's male-dominated environment. There was also the fact that I'd never been to the communities during the strike and the shame I felt about that.

And there was a feeling of doubt about having helped to set up Lesbians Against Pit Closures. But, in the end, the film shows that, in the crucible of class struggle, when unity is necessary, prejudice can disappear in the twinkling of an eye.

JONATHAN BLAKE

The first time I saw the film, I found it really difficult. It brought back all these memories of people who have died. I was meant to be one of them: because of my diagnosis, I never thought I would get to forty and now I've just hit sixty-six. I'm a pensioner and I swim every morning at Brockwell Lido.

PAUL CANNING

I didn't watch the film for ages. I didn't go and see it at the cinema and, when I got a DVD copy, I didn't watch that for ages. One of the reasons was that I have a really hard time dealing with things about HIV. And I know that the film isn't about HIV, but there are all these people in it who are dead. And, when I did eventually watch it, that's the emotion it brought up for me. But I was glad it was made.

CLIVE BRADLEY

It got an awful lot incredibly right. As a film, it's in the broad ballpark of something like *The Full Monty* but much more political. It takes for granted that the strike was right. It's absolutely about the importance of class struggle and solidarity between communities and it's good that this particular act of solidarity will be remembered.

MIKE JACKSON

I think the film struck a chord. I don't think it could have been made ten or twenty years ago. And, ironically, we're now in a situation where we have a government which is worse than Thatcherism. It is naked, blatant, arrogant and cruel. And I think the film came out at a time when people were really frustrated and angry and didn't know what to do. *Pride* showed that grassroots activism – forget the party apparatchiks and the media – can make difference. And that's really heartening.

WENDY CALDON

Talking to young people, I get depressed to discover that they don't know their radical history. It's thirty years on and people don't know about how we used to fight. Whether Tory or Labour, people have become disaffected with politics because they don't feel represented and they've backed away from it. That's why I'm very proud of the film: it showed people that there is a radical social history of people fighting for their rights – and that this needs to go on. And I will always be in awe of the courage of the mining communities during and after the strike.

———

The film's success led to a revival of the activism that drove the young men and women of LGSM – and to the re-birth of the organisation itself.

———

DAVE LEWIS

We re-formed in the aftermath of the film's release and started raising money, primarily for the trust, which was set up in Mark Ashton's name to support people living with HIV and AIDS.

And during that process, we met a range of young people who have become successor groups, which use our LGS-acronym supporting the migrants and the dockers internationally. They have adopted the *'Lesbian and Gays Support'* tag to reference what we did.

MARTIN GOODSELL

Following the film, there was also international interest in what we had done, now [that] there's lots of activism going on, especially with the LGBT community coming out in support of migrants both here in Britain and in Europe. LGSM Migrants group are carrying on in our tradition; and that, to me, is our legacy.

BRETT HARAN

It's incredibly exciting that our story struck a chord and that it has been an inspiration for young people today. Without the film, if someone had told you our story, it would have been dismissed as a bit too far-fetched; as something that would never have happened in real life. But people have been so amazed to find that it is true that they have been inspired and have been given impetus. They have found that you can make common cause; that there is this thing called solidarity and, out of small beginnings, big things can come.

GETHIN ROBERTS

I've spoken at over sixty screenings now – in Ankara and Istanbul, Mexico City, Beijing and Moscow, in Malmo, Warsaw, Milan and many other places – and the reception for the film is always amazing.

It really resonates with people and often inspires them to offer practical solidarity, whether its Lesbians and Gays Support the Migrants in London, UK or in London, Ontario (as well as in Wales, Brighton and Brussels). There are similar groups in Palermo, Copenhagen and Mexico City and, in Norway, there is a group called Lesbians and Gays Support the Dockers. It's truly inspiring that people are continuing LGSM's legacy.

———

But it was not only the positive parts of the story that found an echo in the wake of *Pride*'s success.

The thirtieth anniversary of the landmark Pride event, when the mining communities of South Wales arrived to march shoulder to shoulder with their gay and lesbian supporters, saw a revival of the in-fighting and arguments which LGSM have fought so hard to overcome.

MIKE JACKSON

The London Pride march has become much less political. Even so, after the movie came out, the committee invited us to lead the parade; to be at the head of the march. But it hadn't counted on the fact that we would want the trades unions to march with us. And, for whatever reason, the committee panicked at that and insisted that it would be just LGSM – a maximum of 200 people – followed by a group of sponsors waving flags of the world. The Labour and trade-union contingent would be completely cut off from us, further back.

DAVE LEWIS

The committee did, initially, agree that we could have a contingent of trade unions immediately following those flags. And then they reneged on that. So it wasn't that they hadn't thought about us being a political group but rather that they went back on a commitment.

MIKE JACKSON

We think that the committee liked the idea of the movie – the glamour, the famous actors. But they hadn't thought about the fact that we were still a political group who would want to make a political point. In the end, the committee wouldn't budge and we decided not to lead the march. As it happened, one of us summed it up by saying, 'We led the march from the middle.'

DAVE LEWIS

The people who control London Pride now get really excited about the fact that they've got the Red Arrows flying over Trafalgar Square. I'm outraged by that. They think that the battles have all been won – and I disagree with that wholeheartedly.

MIKE JACKSON

It's a conundrum: the fact is that, through generations fighting for change and improving the lot of the LGBT community, there's nowhere near as much to fight for today. And I think that's why the Pride march has been almost deliberately de-politicised and turned into a carnival.

DAVE LEWIS

Huge advances have been made and there have been legal changes: it is much easier to live your life as whoever you are in London or Manchester or Birmingham. But you go to Skegness or Oldham, or somewhere like that, and it's a very, very different kettle of fish.

And I think that there's still a bleeding wound in many people's hearts that the miners strike was a defeat. And a defeat to the extent that it was. Thatcher and the Tories had to pull out every available stop but I think that the victory was allowed to happen by some of the people on our own side.

I don't think that the trade-union membership – the rank-and-file membership – is blameless. They weren't applying sufficient pressure on the leadership. That's a lesson that needs to be remembered.

PRIDE

If anyone reading this still believes that the British State is liberal, plural, benign or paternal, please look to see just how that State machine was treating the striking miners in 1984. And then take our story with you into future battles – because you need to know what you're up against in order to stand a chance at victory.

AFTERWORD

In May 1945 Aneurin Bevan MP – the son of a South Wales miner and who, two months later, would become Minister of Health in the Labour government that nationalised Britain's mines – wrote in the *Daily Herald*, 'This island is made mainly of coal and surrounded by fish. Only an organising genius could produce a shortage of coal and fish at the same time.'

Forty years later, the organisational 'genius' of Margaret Thatcher's Conservative government engineered a year-long industrial dispute, which ensured that Britain's vast reserves of coal were abandoned in favour of cheaper imports, while hundreds of thousands of men, women and children in mining communities were deliberately starved into submission.

This was no accident. Mrs Thatcher and her government's friends in big business believed that the market should be the sole and final arbiter. No matter that closing pits destroyed lives and devastated communities: private profit outweighed public benefit. And so Britain's coalfields had to be shut down, and the families which depended upon them had to be abandoned without so much as a backward glance.

Yet today – more than thirty years after the 1984–85 miners' strike – Britain still relies on coal to create almost ten per cent of the electricity we need to power industry and our homes.

And, although the valleys of South Wales – let alone the rich seams of the English midlands – still have enough coal in them to supply power stations for many decades, rather than reopen those pits, the privatised industry imports stocks from across the globe. It was – it is – the economics of the madhouse.

No government since has made a true calculation of the price of this wholesale vandalism. Such estimates as exist[15] put the overall cost – first for benefits, then for social decay and deprivation (let alone the unearned taxes) – at more than £28 billion.

This book was researched and written in one of the most turbulent twelve months in living memory. The year 2016 saw the rise of an inchoate and angry populism: a dark tide which brought in its wake a toxic swell of racism, xenophobia and barely contained violence, which culminated in Britain's decision to leave the European Union, as well as the election of Donald Trump to the US Presidency. Not since the tumultuous year of 1984–85 has the world been so divided by hatred, or seemed so volatile and so threatening.

---

[15] Notably, the calculations of the late David Feickert, the NUM's research officer from 1983–93.

AFTERWORD

However ugly, however ill-reasoned, some of the anger and division of these past twelve months is a much-delayed reaction to the price we are continuing to pay for Mrs Thatcher's free-market economics and the decades of casino capitalism which followed.

This year has, more than most, then, brought home the need to heed and remember our history. And while that history is dominated by the vicious, cynical and short-term politics which led to the 1984–85 miners' strike, it also includes the generosity and selflessness of those who fought so hard to protect its victims.

The story of LGSM, and the relationship built between the vibrant young gay men and women of London and the beleaguered villages of the South Wales coalfield, is not simply a heart-warming story or an oddity from history. It is, in these fractured times especially, a vital reminder of how common cause may always be found if only we break down the barricades of prejudice.

I feel immensely privileged to have been trusted with the stories of the men and women of LGSM and those of the communities in the Neath, Dulais and Upper Swansea Valleys. And I hope that the telling of them may lead to a resurgence of the courage, kindness and solidarity with which each of these ostensibly very different communities sustained the other.

Because now, more than ever, we need them.

Tim Tate
Wiltshire, December 2016

FURTHER READING

For those wishing to undertake further exploration, there are two remarkable archives of contemporary documents.

The first – 'The Coalfield Collections at Swansea University' – hold the records of the Neath, Dulais and Upper Swansea Valley Support Group. These chronicle the extraordinary achievements of that organization throughout the 1984–85 strike.

The second is maintained by LGSM itself. As the group's secretary, Mike Jackson was a diligent note-taker and record-keeper. At some point during the early months of its existence, Mark Ashton instructed Mike to keep all LGSM's documents safe for posterity. The group's current website – http://lgsm. org/ – is a fine place for committed readers to begin their own journey, and also has contact details that will assist with enquiries to consult LGSM's formidable archive.

For further research, I can recommend the following works, which provide much more contextual material than this book can encompass:

History on Our Side: Wales and the 1984–85 Miners' Strike
Hywel Francis, Lawrence & Wishart, 2015

Mrs Hellfire – The Life and Endeavours of Hefina Headon
Jayne D. Headon (Jayne Francis-Headon), Headon Publishing, 2015

Marching to the Fault Line: The Miners' Strike and the Battle for Industrial Britain
Francis Beckett and David Hencke, Constable, 2009

How Black Were Our Valleys
Deborah Price and Natalie Butts-Thompson, BBTS Publications, 2013

Over the Rainbow: Money, Class and Homophobia
Nicola Field, Dog Horn Publishing, 2016

Gay in the 80s: From Fighting for Our Rights to Fighting for Our Lives
Colin Clews, Troubador Publishing, 2017

Walking after Midnight: Gay Men's Life Stories
The Hall-Carpenter Archives, Routledge, 1989

The Oldest Gay in the Village
George Montague, John Blake Publishing, 2014